T0101946

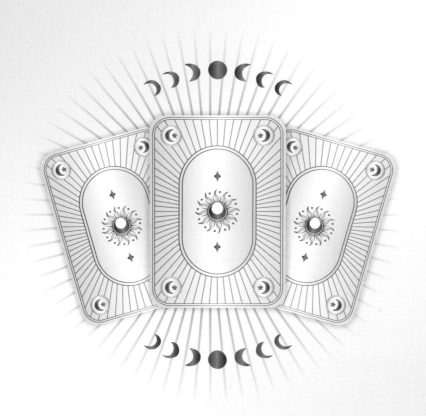

ORACLE CARD
COMPANION

ORACLE CARD

COMPANION

MASTER THE ART OF CARD READING

VICTORIA MAXWELL

ROCKPOOL

A Rockpool book
PO Box 252
Summer Hill
NSW 2130
Australia

rockpoolpublishing.com
Follow us! f ⃝ rockpoolpublishing
Tag your images with #rockpoolpublishing

ISBN: 9781922785374

Published in 2023 by Rockpool Publishing
Copyright text © Victoria Maxwell 2023
Copyright images and design © Rockpool Publishing 2023

Photography by Leah Ladson, leahladson.com
(except images on pages 171, 190, 207 and 209)

All rights reserved. No part of this publication may be reproduced, stored in
a retrieval system, or transmitted in any form or by any means, electronic,
mechanical, photocopying, recording or otherwise, without the prior written
permission of the publisher.

Design and typsetting by Sara Lindberg, Rockpool Publishing
Edited by Lisa Macken

A catalogue record for this
book is available from the
National Library of Australia

Printed and bound in China
10 9 8 7 6 5 4 3 2 1

CONTENTS

INTRODUCTION

How would you like to sit down for a chat with a higher power or with the highest part of yourself that just *knows*? Are you interested in receiving quick, simple answers to the questions that keep you awake at night? How about getting some clear guidance on the situations that are causing you stress and worry? Do you want to know which decision to make or the best next step to take? Would you be keen on just generally living life with more trust, ease and *knowing,* fully embodying your purpose and power?

If you answered 'Yes' to any of the above you are in the right place, because this book is going to show you exactly how to do all of that with nothing but a deck of oracle cards!

I've always been fascinated by divination, the idea that we can communicate with the divine or access our deepest inner knowing through tools, symbols or random objects. In primary school I was obsessed with those paper fortune-tellers where you picked a number and then another number and found out who you'd marry or how many kids you were going to have. I *loved* those things. I don't know that I ever felt like they were really accurate, but some part of me always wondered: *what if it is real?* Then I discovered numerology games, where you'd count the letters in your name and the name of your crush and work out your score out of 100. Weird fact: I used to get 99 per cent with Bart Simpson (#90sKid). In high school I came across another incredible divination tool, the eraser with 'Yes' written on one side and 'No' on the other. All you had to do was throw it in the air while thinking of a question and the eraser would fall and show you the answer. Truly magic – or, at least, it felt like magic when you got the answer you wanted to see!

The first of the more traditional divination tools I worked with was a set of runes. As a teenage witch I really wanted them to be my thing because they felt so witchy and mysterious. The only problem was that they were just as mysterious to me, as I could never remember the names of the symbols or what they meant.

Still desperate to communicate with the universe, in my early 20s I bought my first tarot deck. Like my situation with the runes I really struggled for a long time to figure out what the tarot cards were trying to tell me. Eventually, I fell in love with the tarot system and became a professional tarot reader but it was a relationship that took time, effort, sweat and occasional tears.

I got my first oracle deck around 2011 when I started getting the nudge to become serious about my spiritual journey. I casually added it to an online order of some other magical goodies I was purchasing without thinking too much about it. When the deck arrived I was blown away by how easy it was to use and how accurate the guidance was. That deck helped me navigate through another layer of spiritual awakening and many big transitions in my life. I used it often while I was starting my spiritual blog New Age Hipster, which eventually turned into my full-time business. It was pretty simple, really: I just pulled some cards from my oracle deck, paid attention to the guidance that was coming through, took action and got on a better, more fulfilling and aligned path.

Divination has traditionally been used to see the future, but as we journey on the spiritual path we begin to realise that a paper fortune-teller can't really tell us who we're going to marry and our erasers don't create our fate. We do.

While most of us can pick up an oracle deck and start reading for ourselves within just a few minutes, there is so much more magic to work with in the cards. Created as a tool for divination, oracle cards can also assist you to develop your own intuition and psychic ability, and be used for spiritual healing, energy healing, protection, spellwork, shadow work and lightwork and as a tool for personal transformation and manifestation.

Most importantly, oracle cards can help you live the life of your dreams. I wrote this book not only to support you in becoming a more confident reader, but also to show you how to use your cards to live a more connected, intuitive and magical life with or without a deck in your hands.

I wish you nothing but joy, deep connection, powerful positive transformation and so much magic on this journey!

With so much love,

HOW TO USE
THIS BOOK

Let's get one thing clear right from the start: *there is no right or wrong way to read oracle cards*. There is only the way that works for you, and the way that doesn't. In this book you'll find advice, ideas, rituals and practices that have worked for me and for many of my students and clients over the years.

This book is not an instruction manual: it's a guide to help you on your journey. We are all different, we all read cards differently and we all want different things from our card-reading practice. There may be sections of the book that are perfect for where you are and others that just don't resonate. Maybe you just want to feel more confident reading cards, perhaps you're already a confident or even professional reader and are looking for some new ideas or you might be here just for the plethora of spreads in Chapter 5. It's all good, and it all works. Trust your own intuition and follow your own path, and use this book in whatever way you feel called to.

If you are brand new to card reading you may like to work your way through the book cover to cover or begin with Chapter 6, which will help kick-start your journey.

You can work with this book using absolutely any oracle deck you already own, but if you don't yet own a deck you can find tips on how to choose one in Chapter 1. If you're a bit of a spiritual rebel you can even use a tarot deck. It's also a great idea to work with a journal for deeper insights, and there's more about how to journal with your cards in the section 'Journalling with oracle cards'.

You'll find lots of opportunities called 'Pull a card!' throughout the book. When you see these prompts, grab your cards, prepare for a reading, ask your question or questions and pull a card –

or two, or as many as you like! Take some time to journal on your reading for extra insight. Remember that as you set out on this journey your oracle cards are just a portal that opens into divine guidance and more deeply into your own heart. You are the real oracle.

If you'd like to share your readings and insights with this book, use the hashtag #oraclecardcompanion and tag me so I can come and say 'Hey!' I'm @newagehipster333 on Instagram, Facebook and TikTok.

A BRIEF
HISTORY OF
DIVINATION

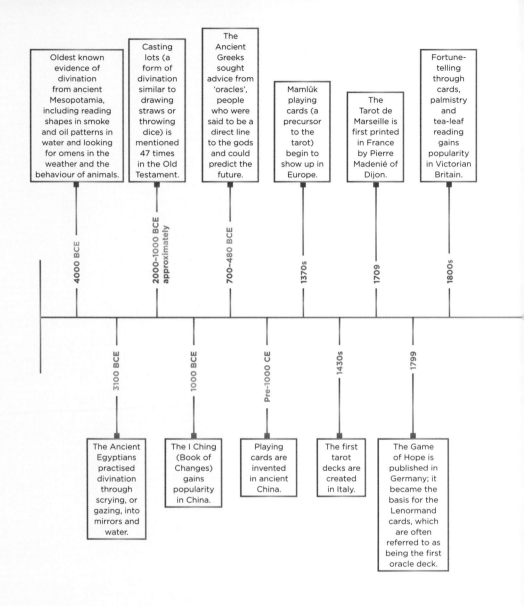

Oldest known evidence of divination from ancient Mesopotamia, including reading shapes in smoke and oil patterns in water and looking for omens in the weather and the behaviour of animals.

Casting lots (a form of divination similar to drawing straws or throwing dice) is mentioned 47 times in the Old Testament.

The Ancient Greeks sought advice from 'oracles', people who were said to be a direct line to the gods and could predict the future.

Mamlūk playing cards (a precursor to the tarot) begin to show up in Europe.

The Tarot de Marseille is first printed in France by Pierre Madenié of Dijon.

Fortune-telling through cards, palmistry and tea-leaf reading gains popularity in Victorian Britain.

4000 BCE

2000–1000 BCE approximately

700–480 BCE

1370s

1709

1800s

3100 BCE

1000 BCE

Pre-1000 CE

1430s

1799

The Ancient Egyptians practised divination through scrying, or gazing, into mirrors and water.

The I Ching (Book of Changes) gains popularity in China.

Playing cards are invented in ancient China.

The first tarot decks are created in Italy.

The Game of Hope is published in Germany; it became the basis for the Lenormand cards, which are often referred to as being the first oracle deck.

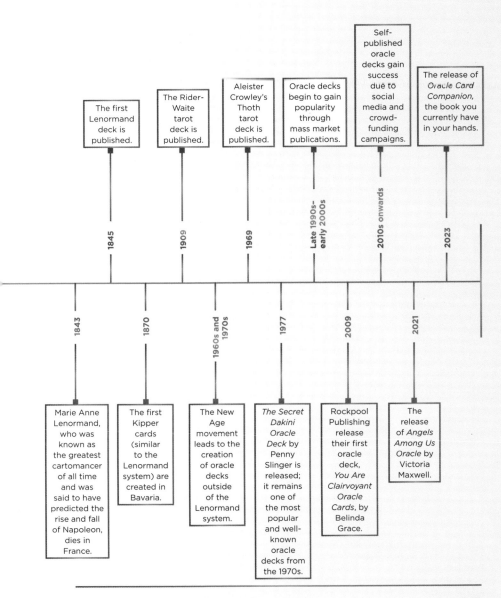

The first Lenormand deck is published.

1845

The Rider-Waite tarot deck is published.

1909

Aleister Crowley's Thoth tarot deck is published.

1969

Oracle decks begin to gain popularity through mass market publications.

Late 1990s-early 2000s

Self-published oracle decks gain success due to social media and crowd-funding campaigns.

2010s onwards

The release of *Oracle Card Companion,* the book you currently have in your hands.

2023

1843

Marie Anne Lenormand, who was known as the greatest cartomancer of all time and was said to have predicted the rise and fall of Napoleon, dies in France.

1870

The first Kipper cards (similar to the Lenormand system) are created in Bavaria.

1960s and 1970s

The New Age movement leads to the creation of oracle decks outside of the Lenormand system.

1977

The Secret Dakini Oracle Deck by Penny Slinger is released; it remains one of the most popular and well-known oracle decks from the 1970s.

2009

Rockpool Publishing release their first oracle deck, *You Are Clairvoyant Oracle Cards,* by Belinda Grace.

2021

The release of *Angels Among Us Oracle* by Victoria Maxwell.

A brief history of divination

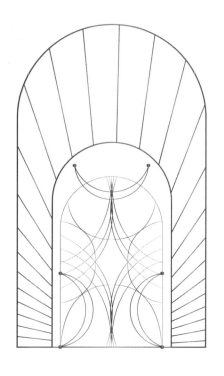

JOURNALLING WITH ORACLE CARDS

As you work through this book you'll notice lots of invitations to journal to help you dive a little deeper. It's always fun to buy a new journal when you're starting on a fresh adventure, but you can use any notebook you already have even if it's half full of something else or even create a journal on your computer. The best way to journal is however it is going to work for you and your personal preferences and lifestyle.

JOURNALLING CAN:

+ help you remember things you're sure you'll remember in the moment but will probably forget later on
+ support you to go deeper with the information and exercises in this book
+ help you receive expanded, more meaningful messages through your oracle readings
+ highlight common threads and lessons that are coming up for you
+ give you an opportunity to go back later and see how far you've come
+ capture all the gold nuggets of wisdom that come through
+ show you how on point your intuition and readings were after things unfolded
+ provide more clarity and depth to your readings than just reading the guidebook that comes with the cards
+ help you to figure things out.

IN ORDER TO GET THE MOST OUT OF USING A JOURNAL ALONGSIDE THIS BOOK:

✦ take notes on anything and everything

✦ answer any journal prompts in as little or as much detail as you like

✦ record your readings and any insights you get from the 'Pull a card!' sections throughout this book

✦ record any thoughts and ideas that come up as you work with the book

✦ Record what works for you and write about what doesn't

✦ keep a page of questions you want guidance on and add to it when a new question comes to mind

✦ keep a note of your readings

✦ whatever else you like!

FOLLOW THESE STEPS TO JOURNAL ON YOUR READINGS:

✦ record the date

  ✦ record the deck you used

    ✦ record the question/s you asked

      ✦ for a one-card reading: record the card you pulled and then all your thoughts, feelings and anything else that comes through

        ✦ if you're using a spread: record your question, the name of the spread, the card position (the number), prompt (the phrase the spread offers), the card you pulled and your thoughts, feelings and any other notes, and do the same for each card in the spread and make some notes on the overall reading.

Go back later and look at your old readings, because you may find some wisdom that's still relevant for you now and it will help you see how much progress you've made on the journey.

If you don't want to or you're not into journalling, still try to find some way of recording your process and what comes up in your readings. You could perhaps take photos of the cards you've pulled or voice record your thoughts, and you may even like to create a social media account that's public or private and just for you in which you share your readings and journey with the cards. If you do publicly share any posts inspired by this book please be sure to tag #oraclecardcompanion so I can find and support you on your journey.

Remember that nothing you write in your journal is set in stone, that it's just a reflection of your thoughts, feelings and card readings in that moment. You will evolve and grow and change your mind, which is all part of the process. Give yourself permission to be where you are right now and to evolve and change as you continue on your oracle card–reading journey.

GENERAL JOURNAL PROMPTS FOR ORACLE-CARD READING

Use all or any of these prompts any time you pull a card to gain deeper insight through journalling:

- ✦ How does this card make you feel?
- ✦ Do you feel any resistance to this card?
- ✦ Are there any uncomfortable emotions or thoughts coming up?
- ✦ What's preventing you from experiencing the best outcome this card could offer?
- ✦ What would life look like if you fully embodied the guidance of this card?
- ✦ What could you do right now to take a step towards or away from this guidance?
- ✦ What longer-term action would you need to take to create the best possible outcome from the guidance on this card?

PREPARING FOR READINGS

In this chapter we will look at how to best prepare yourself in order to receive clear and empowering readings every time.

CHOOSING AN ORACLE DECK

There is no right or wrong way for an oracle deck to come into your life. Although it can be a magical experience when you purchase your first or latest deck, it doesn't have to be. Maybe you fell in love with a deck you'd seen someone else using online or picked one up in a shop and just got a good feeling about it because you liked the colours or the artwork. Perhaps a deck came into your life via someone else gifting it to you.

No matter how a deck comes to you trust it is meant to be, although you can't deny there is a kind of magic in buying a deck from a bricks and mortar shop and especially if it's a witchy or metaphysical shop with a great vibe. You get to take your time browsing and receive recommendations from the staff. Some shops have deck packs open so you can take a good look through the cards or give yourself a quick reading to see if the messages resonate. If you're able to get to a shop to choose a deck there are a few things you can do to support the process.

BEFORE YOU LEAVE HOME AND WALK INTO A SHOP, SET AN INTENTION FOR WHAT YOU'RE LOOKING FOR. INTENTIONS COULD INCLUDE A DECK THAT WILL:

✦ help you form a deeper connection with your guides and angels

✦ help you get on your best and highest path

- ✦ be in alignment with the highest frequencies possible
- ✦ bring you great blessings of comfort, support or guidance
- ✦ help you with whatever is coming up for you specifically at this time.

You may walk into the shop and be instantly guided to the right deck and just *know* it's the one for you. In that case, trust that knowing and head to the register!

WHEN YOU ARE SHOPPING IN PERSON:

- ✦ Hold the deck you're thinking about buying in your non-dominant hand, close your eyes and take a deep breath.
- ✦ Think about the first thing that pops into your head: do any visions, words or phrases come through for you?
- ✦ See if it feels good to hold the deck in your hands.
- ✦ Notice how you feel in your body: do you feel tense, relaxed, happy, at ease or unsure?

If you're unsure about the deck, put it back on the shelf and have a wander around or go for a walk or a coffee. If you're still thinking about the deck it could be a sign to go back and get it, but if you're still not sure it may be a 'No' or a 'Not yet'.

IF YOU CAN'T FIND A DECK YOU LIKE IN A STORE OR DON'T HAVE A STORE TO GO TO, WELL, THERE'S ALWAYS ONLINE SHOPPING! HERE ARE SOME TIPS FOR SHOPPING ONLINE:

✦ As with shopping in store, take a moment to set an intention for what it is you're looking for.

✦ Close all other tabs and windows or at least try not to multitask work, email and social media while you're looking for your perfect deck.

✦ Head to your favourite online bookshop or witchy shop and start browsing.

✦ Notice how you feel as you look at the covers, cards and information online. Let your intuition guide you and pay attention to how you feel when looking at each deck.

✦ Sometimes when you know you know, so trust that feeling.

✦ If you're unsure, wait. If you still feel drawn to the deck days or weeks later it's probably the right one for you, but if it no longer seems like the one then keep searching.

Looking for decks online has the added benefit of reviews, unboxing videos and exploring via hashtags. Check out what others are saying about the decks you're interested in, but do remember to always trust your own intuition. What doesn't work for someone else may be the perfect deck for you.

There's something really special about holding a deck of cards in your hands, but using an oracle-card app can absolutely still work for receiving guidance. For the most part this just comes down to preference: if you're technologically inclined you may find an app works better for you than a physical deck, or if you're more old school the idea of pulling cards on an app may not resonate. See what works best for you.

Follow hashtags on social media such as #oraclecards, #oraclecardreadersofinstagram or #rockpoolpublishing to discover new oracle decks, or ask your oracle card–reading friends for deck suggestions. You don't have to take them on board, but it can be a great place to start. Decision paralysis and feeling overwhelmed can be real at times, especially when we're presented with so many beautiful decks. There is absolutely nothing wrong with just using whatever deck is available.

If a deck no longer works for you, you can always gift it to a friend or donate, sell or swap it; there are loads of groups on Facebook where you can do a deck swap. You can also use the cards as prayer cards or bookmarks or in art projects. Don't let the pressure of looking for the perfect deck stop you from getting started.

Second-hand decks

There is a belief in card-reading communities that you shouldn't use a second-hand deck as they contain the energy of the people who used them before you. There are also some people who won't let anyone else touch their cards for the same reason. However, if you cleanse, activate and bond with a second-hand deck in the ways described in the next section there is no reason why a previously used deck can't work just as well for you as a brand-new one.

CLEARING, ACTIVATING AND CHARGING YOUR ORACLE DECK

There are many different ways to clear and activate your deck once you get it home. You may like to start by clearing your deck of any energy it has picked up in the printing and distribution process or from the shop you purchased it in before you start doing readings.

The following are some traditional methods to clear your deck you can use before you work with your deck for the first time and any time you feel your deck needs cleansing. You may like to cleanse your deck periodically, on a new or full moon, after you've done some big readings, after someone else has touched your cards or any time you feel the messages are getting murky, sluggish or tired. To clear your oracle deck you can use any of these methods:

✦ Hold the deck in your non-dominant hand and tap it with the knuckles of your dominant hand to knock out any negativity and old energy.

✦ Tap the edge or edges of the deck on a table.

✦ Blow or breathe onto your deck, which is a quick way to cleanse but also bond the deck with your energy.

✦ Waft incense or the smoke from ethically sourced palo santo or sage around and through the cards. When doing this, separate the cards to make sure the smoke touches every card in the deck.

✦ Place crystals on your deck to cleanse it. The best crystals for this are clear quartz and selenite. Wash your clear quartz afterwards and cleanse your selenite with sound or smoke.

✦ Play singing bowls, bells or tingshas (small cymbals) over or near your deck to clear it with sound.

✦ Hold your deck in your non-dominant hand, place your dominant hand just above the deck and visualise reiki healing energy or a violet flame of light clearing through the cards.

✦ Place your deck on a pile of salt and sprinkle salt around and on top of it. Make sure the salt is completely dry.

✦ Use a very light misting of any type of aura spray over your deck. Separate all the cards and lay them on the ground or a large table and gently mist over the cards. Be very careful when using this technique, as too much water can warp the cards.

✦ Sunlight works well for both clearing and charging. Again, be careful to place the deck somewhere dry while it clears in the sunlight and don't leave it for too long or the colours may fade.

✦ Rub a diluted essential oil of your choosing onto your hands. Any cleansing oil works well; try sage, peppermint, rosemary or eucalyptus. Wait until the oil is slightly absorbed into your skin and then give your deck a shuffle. Again, be very careful with this method as you don't want your deck to get oily.

✦ One of the best ways to clear your deck is simply by shuffling the cards. You can find out more about different ways to shuffle in Chapter 2.

✦ Reorder the cards, as putting them back into their original order is a great way to reset the deck.

Activating your oracle deck

Once your deck is clear it's time to activate and bond with the cards. Activating your deck is a little like charging it, turning it on or waking it up. One of the simplest ways to activate your deck is by slowly going through it, looking at and touching each card, which will put your energy into every card in the deck. You could also try this ritual to activate your deck:

✦ Clear the deck by knocking it three times with your knuckles or gently knocking the edge of the deck on a table or flat surface.

✦ Hold the deck to your heart and take a deep breath.

✦ Take a few further deep breaths and visualise a golden white light opening up and expanding in and around your heart, filling the cards with the light from your own heart.

✦ Say out loud or in your head:

> *'Thank you, cards, for coming into my life. Thank you for being a powerful tool for guidance, support, healing and transformation. Thank you for helping me to connect more deeply with my own heart, my intuition, my higher self, my guides and angels and all beings from the highest realms of love, light, peace and truth who guide me. Thank you for being a part of my spiritual journey and for helping me to live more deeply, more truthfully, more powerfully and more peacefully. Thank you that every reading done with these cards will always be in alignment with love, light, my best and highest good*

and the best and highest good of those I read for. And
so it is.'

✦ Go through the cards, touching each one while holding the intention that this deck will help you receive the guidance you most need.

✦ Pull a card and see what the first message this deck has for you is. Put the card back in the deck, shuffle it and then place it on your altar with a crystal on top, or put it back in the box and keep it somewhere safe.

Charging your oracle deck

Charging your deck is similar to keeping your phone charged: you want the energy to stay topped up so you can grab your deck any time and get the guidance you need. To charge your deck:

✦ Place a crystal on top of the deck, either in or out of the box, when you're not using it to keep its energy high vibe and happy. Amethyst is a favourite of many card readers as it is a very clearing, grounding and intuitive stone. You may like to use smoky quartz for protection, selenite or angelite for high angelic frequencies or clear quartz as a general all-purpose stone.

✦ Keep your deck on your altar or sacred space, letting it rest and charge there until you are ready to use it again.

✦ Charge your deck at the time of a full or new moon. A full moon brings in energy of releasing, healing, letting go, gratitude and presence while a new moon is better suited for fresh beginnings and manifestation. Consider the energy and sign of the current moon before letting your deck charge, as some full moons are particularly intense. If the moon is making you feel exhausted or a little strange it could do the same to your deck. A word to the wise: avoid charging your decks or crystals during an eclipse.

✦ Breathe on your deck so that you can clear, charge and connect with it quickly.

CARING FOR YOUR ORACLE DECK

How you store your deck is really up to you and will depend on your lifestyle, who you share a home with and how many decks you have. There is an old tarot tradition that says the best way to store a deck is to take it out of the box it came in, wrap it in a silk scarf and keep it in a wooden box. This isn't such a great way of storing decks if you have more than a few, like to travel with them, want to be able to grab one quickly when you have a burning question or if you're vegan (silk isn't vegan friendly)!

The idea really is just to store your decks in a respectful way, because how you treat your decks can be a mirror to how they treat you. As a general rule, try not to throw them around, leave them under piles of junk, let the dog eat them, forget them in the bottom of your bag for months on end and so on. Of course, leaving them in your bag during the week so you can do readings on your lunch break is totally fine.

Keeping your cards on a bookshelf or in a drawer if you're hiding them from people in your home who don't get your new interest is a perfectly good way to store your decks. Trust your intuition and look after your decks in whatever way feels right for you. Just remember to treat them nicely, and they'll be good to you.

BONDING WITH YOUR ORACLE DECK

Bonding with your deck is all about learning how it communicates with you. Like any relationship, the more time and effort you put into getting to know one another the easier it will be to connect and understand each other. Some ways you can bond with your deck include the following:

✦ Carry your deck around with you. It may sound a little strange, but having your deck in your aura for a while can help create a strong bond.

✦ Sleep with it under your pillow or on your bedside table.

✦ Use it! Pull at least one card for yourself each day. You may find it useful to keep your deck next to the kettle or by your bedside so you have a reminder to pull a card first thing in the morning and/or last thing at night.

✦ Go through the deck slowly and record in your journal your thoughts and feelings about each card. This is a wonderful way to start developing your intuition.

✦ Let your deck settle in and hang out in your space for a while. Put it on a shelf with your other decks and let it get used to you.

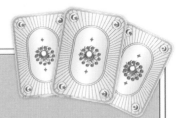

Pull a card!

Take a few deep breaths and relax. With your deck face up, go through and choose the card you like most then choose the card you like the least. Record in your journal the answers to these questions for both cards:

+ What is it that you like most/least about this card (colour, image, keywords and so on)?
+ How does this card make you feel?
+ Does this card bring up any memories?
+ Where in your body do you feel this card?
+ Does this card remind you of a person in your life?
+ What situation in your life could this card relate to?

Interview with your deck spread

Another fun way to bond with your deck is to do an interview spread.

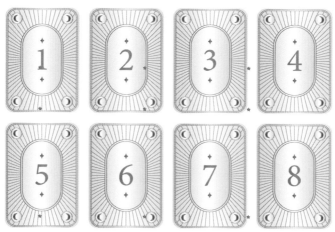

ASK YOUR DECK THESE QUESTIONS:

✦ What have you come into my life to help me with?

✦ What kinds of questions are you best able to answer?

✦ Do you have any limitations?

✦ How can you help me grow?

✦ What can you teach me?

✦ How can we bond?

✦ How would you like to be looked after?

✦ How can we communicate effectively?

It can sometimes take a while to bond with a deck. Just like when you meet someone for the first time, sometimes you click straight away while at other times you have to know someone for a while before you really warm to each other. You may find you are very drawn to a deck, get it home and then leave it sitting on a shelf for six months before you suddenly get an urge to start using it. It then becomes your favourite deck.

Don't give up on your decks, but don't try to force a relationship if it's not working either. Give it time: let your deck settle into your space and try again later.

Another reason we struggle to bond with our decks is because our own energy isn't clear. In the remainder of this chapter we will look at some ways you can prepare yourself and your energy for a reading that will help you feel more clear, grounded and able to connect more easily.

WHO AND WHAT YOU ARE CONNECTING WITH IN A READING

Getting clear on the one small thing of who and what you are connecting with when you use oracle cards can make a huge difference when it comes to getting clearer readings. It can take your readings from being a bit of fun or a quiet moment of introspection with your morning coffee to a deeper connection with the divine.

It's so simple, yet many people never think about this aspect of card reading. How often do you hear phrases such as 'I'll ask the cards' or 'The cards told me . . .'? It's not really the cards that are speaking to you; it's who or what you are connecting with *through* the cards that is giving you the guidance.

While oracle cards certainly do feel magical, they really are just tools. Okay, magical tools for sure, but tools all the same. Just as your phone is a tool you use to connect with your friends and family, your oracle cards are a tool you use to connect with a higher source of wisdom. You wouldn't just pick up your phone and start speaking to *it*: first you have to dial the number of who you want to reach, and card reading is similar to that. You can pick up your cards, shuffle them and hope there's someone on the other end of the line who can help you, or you can decide who you want to speak with, set an intention to connect with them and then shuffle your cards, dialling their number and knowing that you are going to have a conversation with the being or energy of your choice.

Who or what you connect with in particular when reading oracle cards really doesn't matter so much; we're all different and we all have our own ideas about how this all works. So who or what can you connect with through your oracle cards? Some people read cards purely from a psychological perspective to tune in to their own subconscious minds, while others with deep spiritual beliefs or connections may call on their spirit guides, angels, gods, goddesses, ancestors and ascended masters or simply divine guidance. There are also those who prefer to think of oracle-card reading as a way of tuning in to their own intuition, a way to connect with their own inner knowing or higher self.

It doesn't matter who or what you connect with, although choosing to connect with an energy or being that is loving is always advisable; it just matters that you know who or what you're calling.

Spirit guides

Your spirit guides are loving spiritual beings who want to guide you on your best and highest path in this lifetime. They are the spirits of those who have lived a life on earth (usually a spiritual one) and have a vested interest in supporting you in this lifetime.

Spirit guides can be your ancestors, people you have known in this life who've passed over, someone you've known in past lives, members of your soul family or those who have been on a similar path to the one you're on. For example, if you're reading this book you may have a guide who was into divination when they were alive. You can have an unlimited number of guides and may never know them all by name. Calling on them by saying 'spirit guides' is enough. Some may stay with you your whole life, but spirit guides often come and go depending on what's happening in your life and what you most need at the time.

Gods and goddesses

You can call on any gods and goddesses you feel an affinity with in your card readings. Gods and goddesses are aspects of source energy. They are non-denominational, so even if you don't identify as Norse, for example, you can still call on the Norse gods and goddesses to help you. You may find you build a connection with one god or goddess in particular for your readings, or you may feel more drawn to call on different gods and goddesses for diverse issues and questions you have.

Angels and archangels

You don't have to be Christian to call on the angels and archangels. In fact, many religions and spiritual paths mention angels or some form of angelic beings that are available to help guide us in our lives. Angels are very easy to work with, especially at the beginning of your journey, as the angelic frequency is very high, loving and supportive. There are different angels to call on depending on what you need. If you're asking about life purpose try Archangel Michael. Call on Archangel Chamuel for matters of the heart or Archangel Ariel for financial questions.

Ascended masters

'Ascended masters' is a term used for highly evolved spiritual beings who lived on earth and who ascended, reached enlightenment and broke free from the cycle of karma and reincarnation. Among the ascended masters are Jesus and the saints, the Buddha and bodhisattvas and many other religious and spiritual people from history who had – and still have! – a positive impact on the world.

Your higher self

Your higher self is your soul self, the part of you that just seems to know even when your human form feels like it has no idea what's going on. Your higher self remembers your past lives and soul contracts and knows the best path for you to walk to achieve all you came here to do. You can call on your higher self by simply saying the words *'I call on my higher self'*, or you can try connecting through the soul star chakra. This is the chakra that sits just above your head, about where your hands would be if you put them in prayer pose above your head. Visualise a glowing ball of light here, and see it opening up and pouring down love and wisdom over you before, during and after your readings.

Your intuition or inner knowing

Your intuition is your gut feeling; that deep inner knowing; the 'I don't know how I know, I just know' feeling. To connect with your intuition during readings you may like to begin by placing a hand on your heart or belly, or one hand on each, and taking a few deep breaths then setting an intention to connect with your own inner being and knowing.

Your ancestors

By calling on your ancestors you will either connect with a group consciousness of beings or with certain individuals who can support your spiritual work. A word to the wise here: just because Uncle Joe passed over it doesn't make him qualified to help you with oracle readings. Only call on specific ancestors to help you if you really want their energy in your space and supporting you in your life, otherwise calling on the collective ancestor energy may be a better choice.

Ancestors are not just limited to blood relations: love lines are sometimes stronger than blood lines. If you are adopted you have twice as many ancestors, as you have been initiated into a second family line. You can also work with and call on the ancestors of the place in which you live and the ancestors of your culture. Ancestors are all those who have gone before you, so you can even call upon the ancestors of all those who have read cards and worked with divination.

As you dive deeper into oracle-card readings you may find that you are calling in a big team to support you and it may get difficult to distinguish between spirit guides, angels, ascended masters or your inner knowing. Perhaps you're having trouble working out who is actually guiding you. It actually doesn't really matter, because as long as you're receiving loving guidance and your readings are helping you to create positive changes in your life it's all good. Using the word 'guides' or the phrase 'guides and angels' are simple, all-encompassing ways to call on those who guide you.

Pull a card!

Who or what would most be in alignment
with your best and highest good to connect with in your
oracle-card readings?

There are many ways to open up the channels of communication, and we'll go into these in more detail in Chapter 3, but here's a very short ritual you can do to get started right now:

✦ Hold your cards in your hands and close your eyes.

✦ Take three deep breaths.

✦ Concentrate on who or what you'd like to connect with.

✦ Say out loud or in your mind: '*Thank you* [whoever you want to connect with] *for being with me as I do this reading and for showing me the cards that will most guide me right now.*'

✦ Ask a more specific question if you wish – for example, 'What do I most need to know about . . . ?' – or you can just ask for general guidance.

✦ Shuffle the cards, then choose the card you most feel drawn to.

✦ Take a moment to sit with the card you pulled and consider how it answers your question and what guidance you are being given.

✦ When you're done, always thank who or whatever it was you called in to help you.

Whenever you read cards, always set an intention for who you'd like to speak with. It helps to form the connection between you and create respect for the process and who or what you're speaking with. Even if you just do this one thing your readings will become so much clearer and stronger as your relationship with whoever or whatever you are calling on grows.

Note: for ease, in this book I've used the word 'guides' to encompass whoever or whatever it is you are calling upon when reading the cards, but feel free to use this interchangeably with intuition, angels, gods/goddesses, inner knowing and so on.

PREPARING YOUR SPACE

You can read oracle cards anywhere and everywhere, but it can bring another level to your readings if you have a space specifically dedicated to them. Setting up an altar or sacred space is all about doing what works for you, your lifestyle and the place you live. Perhaps you're able to create a reading space with an altar, candles, crystals and cushions in a corner of a room where you won't be disturbed, or maybe your sacred space is a chair out on your back porch, the edge of your bed or even the kitchen table.

What makes a sacred space sacred is your intention. Coming back to the same place each time you do your readings can help to activate a positive energetic imprint in the space and within yourself. It also makes it easier each time you come back to ground and centre yourself, as you'll quickly remember how it feels to sit there and open up to guidance.

A quick and easy way to prepare the space no matter where you are is through using a reading cloth, which can be anything from a purposely designed altar, a reading cloth from a New Age store or simply a scarf or bandanna. As you lay out your reading cloth, set the intention that you are ready to read the cards and connect with your guides.

Lighting a candle is another great way to prepare your reading space. Light the candle with the intention that you're going to connect with your own inner and divine light. Candlelight can also represent the light you would like to have shone on your questions: imagine that light clearing away the darkness and illuminating your path ahead. Other ways to prepare your space can include lighting some herbs or incense, placing a crystal on your reading cloth or spritzing an aura spray around the space.

If you work with an altar or sacred space, be sure to clear the space often. You can do this by removing anything on your altar, dusting and clearing the surface and cleansing any crystals then replacing them in your space. Other ways to clear your space include burning incense, sage or palo santo, spraying or diffusing essential oils, visualising your space filled with white light or a violet flame or just asking your guides to come in and clear the space for you.

All of this can help you get into the right space for your oracle reading, but none of it is essential. As long as you have your cards you can do a reading anywhere and at any time. Remember: you are the altar!

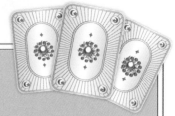

Pull a card!

How can you best prepare your space for a reading?

Use this simple ritual:

✦ Physically clear and clean your space: don't sit in a pile of dirty laundry or read on a dusty table.

✦ Energetically clear your space: light some incense or herbs and waft them around the space, spritz an aura spray or visualise white light clearing through the space.

✦ Set the space: set your reading cloth down, light a candle, play some relaxing high vibrational music, place your crystals around you and get comfortable.

✦ Hold your cards in your hands and prepare your energy (see the next section for more information).

PREPARING YOUR ENERGY

Being relaxed, grounded and centred before you start is a surefire way to get a clearer, more grounded reading. Just as you may not be in the best place to communicate with a partner or friend when you're angry, frustrated, overemotional, unfocused or distracted, it's also not always the best time to do an oracle reading for yourself. However, the good news is that there are plenty of ways you can clear, adjust and align your energy and get into the right energetic place and head space for oracle readings.

Clearing your energy

Energy-clearing practices can help you release any negativity you've picked up that's been sent to you or that you've created within yourself. These practices, such as the ones listed below, also give you a chance to clear and release anything that isn't yours:

+ Visualise white light coming down into your crown chakra at the top of your head and then moving down through your chakra column, down your legs and into your feet. Visualise the white light expanding all around you and clearing your entire auric field.

+ Visualise a violet flame clearing your energy fields, which is a powerful spiritual energy of transmutation. Ask that the violet flame energy clears through all layers of your physical, mental, emotional and etheric bodies and all layers of your auric fields. You can call on Saint Germain to assist with this if you wish.

+ Waft incense or smoke from sage or palo santo through your aura.

+ Indulge in a salt bath.

+ Have a shower.

+ Wash your hands.

+ Take long, deep breaths.

- ✦ Ask Archangel Zadkiel to gently clear you with his angelic light.
- ✦ Clear yourself with sound using tingshas, bells, singing bowls, crystal bowls or recordings.
- ✦ Dance it out or do something to move your body.
- ✦ Practise a yogic breath of fire by inhaling and exhaling evenly, quickly and powerfully.
- ✦ Affirm by saying *'I am clear'* three times.

Protecting your energy

Protecting your energy is an essential practice no matter what you are doing on the spiritual path. Protecting your energy before a reading is simply an intention that nothing can come into your space or into your reading that is not from the highest wisdom or from love. Energy protection also helps you avoid tuning in to anyone else's influence, problems or desires during your readings. You can protect your energy in any of the following ways:

- ✦ Visualise a bubble of white or blue light around your aura like a force field that is protecting your energy.
- ✦ Wear a protection amulet such as a pentagram, cross, ankh or any other protective symbol.
- ✦ Hold or wear a protective crystal. Smoky quartz, black onyx, black tourmaline or anything dark are great for protection.
- ✦ Ask your guides to protect you in your space.
- ✦ Call on Archangel Michael for his protection.
- ✦ Visualise a circle of light around you on the floor.

+ Mist a protective aura spray around you and your space.
+ Affirm by saying *'I am protected'* three times before you begin.

Grounding your energy

It's difficult to make sense of a reading when your energy is not grounded. You'll know you're ungrounded when there are lots of thoughts and energy flying in all different directions or when you're unable to focus. Being ungrounded can be one of the biggest blocks to getting a clear reading. If your energy is all over the place then guess what: your readings will be also. Grounding practices are all about getting back into your body and into the present moment so you can receive the guidance you need. You can ground your energy in any of the following ways:

+ Go outside and reconnect with nature.
+ Get your bare feet on the earth: sand, grass, dirt or whatever you have access to.
+ Eat your veggies, especially root veggies and dark leafy greens.
+ Hug a tree.
+ Visualise roots growing out of the bottoms of your feet and into the earth beneath you.
+ Activate your earth star chakra, which is the energy centre that sits underneath your feet and in the earth beneath you. Visualise this ball of light shining brightly and keeping you anchored.

✦ Carry or wear dark or earthy-toned crystals. Any of the protection crystals (smoky quartz, black onyx, black tourmaline or anything dark) also work well for grounding, or you can try moss or tree agate or petrified wood.

✦ Affirm by saying *'I am grounded'* three times.

Setting an intention

Once your energy is aligned it's time to set an intention, a process that can be as elaborate or as simple as you like.

Pause, take a breath and ask yourself: 'Why am I doing this reading for myself today and what do I want to experience or achieve in doing this?' This isn't the same as asking your specific questions, which we will get into in the next chapter. Setting your intention is just an extra step in making sure you're in a good, aligned and clear place before you start asking questions. Your intention could be:

✦ for positive transformation in your life

✦ to walk your best and highest path

✦ to connect more deeply with your heart and/or inner guidance

✦ to practise and develop your intuition

✦ to connect with the unconditional love of the divine

✦ that everything that comes through in the reading is in alignment with your best and highest good.

PUTTING IT ALL TOGETHER

TRY THIS SIMPLE RITUAL TO PREPARE YOURSELF FOR A READING:

✦ *Clear*: close your eyes and take a few deep breaths. Visualise a golden white light moving through you and all around you. Affirm by saying *'I am clear'* three times.

✦ *Protect*: visualise a bright blue shield of protective light all around you. Affirm by saying *'I am protected'* three times.

✦ *Ground*: visualise roots growing out of your feet and into the earth below you. Affirm by saying *'I am grounded'* three times.

✦ *Call in your guides*: thank your guides or whatever you are calling on for being with you as you do this reading.

✦ *Set an intention*: state your intention; for example, 'May everything that comes through in this reading be in alignment with my best and highest good.'

NOTES

NOTES

CARD-READING
BASICS

As you work with the cards you'll find your own personal ways to shuffle, pull and read them, but if you're new to card reading or just want some new ideas this chapter will provide you with everything you need to get started.

SHUFFLING YOUR CARDS

There are many different ways to shuffle your cards, but it's all about figuring out what works for you. Some popular shuffling methods include:

✦ **Waterfall or overhand shuffle:** hold your deck in your non-dominant hand, then lift up sections from the bottom of the deck and place them on the top of the deck with your other hand.

✦ **Riffle or casino shuffle:** this style of shuffling involves splitting the deck, holding half the cards in each hand and then riffling the corners of each half of the deck together before pushing the cards back into a single deck, cutting again and repeating the process. This very effective shuffling technique can cause your cards to get dog-eared.

✦ **Piling shuffle:** cut the deck, make piles (usually three) then place the piles back together in a different order. Keep going until you feel the cards are adequately shuffled.

✦ **Smooshing:** this is a really fun and effective way to shuffle. Spread your cards out on a table or the floor and then start smooshing or swirling them around in all directions before bringing them back into a single deck.

CHOOSING YOUR CARDS

Figuring out which cards to pick or pull is an intuitive process that will become easier each time you read for yourself. A simple way to know which card to pull for your reading is to work with the waterfall shuffle. Focus on your question, and as you're shuffling wait for a card to stick out of the deck then pull that card for your reading.

Another way to pull cards is by spreading the deck out in a fan shape on your reading cloth. Let your hand hover over the cards until you sense a card that feels different somehow or until one catches your eye. You can also shuffle your cards until you intuitively feel you're done and then pick the top or bottom card from the deck.

Jumping cards

Jumping cards are the ones that just fly right out of the deck while you're shuffling. There are many different beliefs about what these cards mean, but again it's all about letting your intuition guide you. Usually, if a card jumps out it wants your attention. When this happens you can either take that card as the guidance you were asking for, place it into your spread or put it aside for extra guidance on your reading. If two or more cards jump out it could be to get your attention, or it may be that you're not shuffling very well or your energy isn't grounded.

You can always put a jumping card back in the deck and shuffle again. You may be surprised, though, just how many times a jumping card will reappear in your readings when you do put it back in the deck!

PLACING YOUR CARDS

Traditionally, oracle cards are shuffled and chosen face down and then placed face down in a reading or spread. When reading more than one card at a time you have the choice of turning all the cards over at once so you can see everything in the spread before looking at each card in more detail, or you can turn one card over at a time. For beginners it's usually best to use the latter method and then look at how the cards work together.

ASKING QUESTIONS

Asking clear questions is the best way to get clear answers, and asking empowering questions is the best way to get empowering guidance!

Many people read cards using 'should' questions – 'Should I do this?' or 'Should I do that?' – but asking what you should and shouldn't do can be deeply disempowering. Rephrasing your questions in a more empowering way could look like 'What do I most need to know about taking this action?', 'How could taking this action serve me?' or even 'What do I need to be aware of when taking this action?'

There is so much nuance in the word 'should'. When you ask if you should do something, should according to what or whom? How about we rephrase the question and ask 'Is taking this action in alignment with my best and highest good?' and see what comes through from there.

It's also important to try to avoid leading questions, which you might find yourself doing when you know what you want the outcome of the reading to be and are just looking for confirmation. For example, 'Will I get this really awesome job that's absolutely perfect for me?' is a leading question. You're not giving your guides an opportunity to let you know that there might be a better choice because you're already dead set on a particular one. A way to reframe this could be 'What do I need to know about the job I've applied for?' or 'Is this new job in alignment with my best and highest good?'

One question professional readers hear often is something along the lines of 'Should I break up with my boyfriend?' You'll notice that 'Should' in there, and there's also a focus on breaking up as the outcome to the situation. A different way to phrase this could be 'What do I need to know about my relationship with my boyfriend?', 'Is this relationship really supporting me?', 'How can I improve this relationship?' or 'What does this relationship have to teach me?'

Another thing you can do is get tangled up in your question to the point where it becomes a stream of consciousness of many different thoughts about a bunch of various things. Asking one distinct question at a time is the best way to get clear guidance. If you have many things going on in your life that you want guidance on, start with one and then move on to the next thing with a new reading. If you don't know where to start you can always just do a general reading and ask for the guidance that will most help you at this time.

You can ask just about anything with this question template: *'What do I most need to know about* [a particular situation]*?'*

ORACLE CARD COMPANION

If you don't have a specific question you can always ask: 'What do I most need to know right now?'

PREDICTIVE READINGS

Predictive readings, or fortune-telling, has been a very popular form of divination in the past, but times are changing and we're much more aware these days of just how much power we have to manifest and create our future.

Oracle cards can be used to help us look ahead, but as soon as we start asking to know what will happen to us in life we lose our power. Seeing an outcome appear in a reading that we don't want can cause anxiety, fear and hopelessness, with the worst-case scenario being that we actually end up manifesting this outcome through our own beliefs and subconscious actions. If we're not careful, predictive readings can end up becoming self-fulfilling prophecies.

There are still, however, empowering ways to look at what's ahead of you. For example, you could ask 'If I keep going on this path, what is the most likely outcome?' You don't always need to be psychic to figure this out: if you stay in an unhappy relationship and don't make any changes the most likely outcome is that you'll stay unhappy, or if you go for a dream job you're much more likely to actually land it than if you don't even apply.

You can also ask for a potential outcome, which can show you what *may* happen. Just remember you have the power to change this if you don't like what you see.

When you sit down to read cards you bring yourself with you, which is why it's so important to prepare your energy beforehand.

Predictive readings often just show you where you are right now and where you could go from there, so if you sit down to read when you're feeling miserable you may be more likely to see a miserable outcome. As soon as you shift your energy back into alignment or make a different decision the path you're on can change, and so too can your outcome.

Whether or not you decide to do predictive readings for yourself is totally up to you. Some people do find predictions helpful, like getting a heads-up or knowing what to look out for or change to avoid something they don't want. Other people prefer to use their oracle cards as a way to look at the here and now and make their own plans for the future. The best way to figure out what works for you is to try different things.

If you do decide to do predictive readings, just don't forget your power. You have the power to change your fate.

NOTES

NOTES

GUIDANCE
DURING
READINGS

Understanding and developing your intuitive or psychic ability can take your readings from a simple one-word answer to a question to a whole world of information, connection, support and guidance each time you pull a card.

We are all born into this world as intuitive psychic beings, but along the way we often forget how to work with these parts of ourselves. Awakening a bit of psychic ability doesn't necessarily mean you'll start seeing visions of the future, and as you know you have the power to change your future. Becoming more psychic is just another way to say you're more aware, awake, conscious and connected to the universe, the divine and your inner knowing.

Whether you know it or not, you're already intuitive and psychic. You may have had experiences in which you just *knew* what decision to make, or you felt the urge to reach out to a friend without knowing they were going through something really difficult. Maybe you knew who was calling before the phone rang or narrowly avoided a bad situation.

When you start to acknowledge, activate and awaken these sleeping parts of yourself, one of the most difficult parts of the process is figuring out the difference between intuition or divine guidance and making it up. The simple answer to this problem is to practise, because the more you work with your oracle cards the more you will start to understand how your intuition and guidance speak to you.

In this chapter we're going to look at the clairs – the different ways you can receive guidance or connect with your intuition – and explore some ways to practise and develop each of them. You can develop all of the clairs, but you may find that just one or two work best for you. Consider the situations below.

Which of the following are you more likely to say?

✦ 'I see what you mean' (clairvoyance).

✦ 'I hear what you're saying' (clairaudience).

✦ 'I feel you' (clairsentience).

✦ 'I understand' or 'I get you' (claircognisance).

WHEN PLANNING A HOLIDAY DO YOU:

✦ Visualise yourself already there and see yourself doing all the things you want to do (clairvoyance)?

✦ Listen to podcasts, watch YouTube videos of people talking about their own trips or listen to music from the place you want to go to (clairaudience)?

✦ Think about how good it's going to be: you can almost feel the sunshine on your face or the warm water all around you as you swim (clairsentience)?

✦ Read articles, check out the history and explore all the information you can find about where you're going (claircognisance)?

WHEN YOU GET A GOOD FEELING ABOUT SOMETHING DO YOU:

✦ See a vision or image in your mind's eye showing you something working out in your favour (clairvoyance)?

✦ Hear an inner voice telling you to go for it (clairaudience)?

✦ Get a good feeling in your gut or start to feel excitement rush through your body (clairsentience)?

+ Just know that something good is going to happen even though you don't know how you know that (claircognisance)?

CLAIRVOYANCE

Clairvoyance means 'clear seeing', and this is the clair people are most familiar with. That doesn't mean it's a better or greater clair, just that it's the most well known. Clairvoyance is the receiving of psychic information through sight or visions. Usually this looks like a movie playing in your mind's eye but it can also include seeing auras, angels, guides and passed-over loved ones either in your mind's eye or out in the physical world.

If you are clairvoyant you may be drawn to certain parts of the images on oracle cards, or as you turn a card over you may see images in your mind's eye of the situation you are asking about or the action steps to take. In your mind's eye you may see signs and symbols, a place, someone you know, a guide who is helping you or even visions of your past lives. Take note of anything that you visualise during a reading, as it may be that you are receiving your guidance clairvoyantly.

TO WAKE UP YOUR CLAIRVOYANCE:

+ Prepare your energy for a reading (see Chapter 1).
+ Close your eyes and get still and quiet in meditation.
+ Open your inner eye, keeping the physical eyes closed, and

visualise a white screen in front of you. Try not to judge or question yourself; just let the images come to the screen. Don't worry if nothing comes or if you see something you don't understand as this is just a process. Record what you saw, and if you didn't see anything try again later.

✦ When you're ready, open your eyes.

TO DEVELOP YOUR CLAIRVOYANCE:

✦ Practise visualisation: look at something in the world around you, then close your eyes and try to visualise it. Including all of the small details.

✦ Close your eyes and visualise your perfect day playing out in front of you.

✦ Read fiction: visualising what you are reading is a great workout for the mind's eye.

✦ Listen to guided meditations that take you on a journey.

✦ Use your imagination.

TRY THIS ORACLE PRACTICE:

✦ Pull an oracle card and notice what part of the image you're most drawn to. Get curious about why you're drawn to that aspect of the image.

✦ Pull an oracle card and notice if any other visions or symbols come to your mind's eye.

✦ Take some notes for your journal.

Pull a card!

Ask these questions:

✦ How can I wake up and activate my clairvoyance?
✦ How am I already using my clairvoyance?
✦ How can I continue to develop and strengthen my clairvoyance?

CLAIRAUDIENCE

Clairaudience means 'clear hearing', and it involves receiving messages through sound in the physical world or with your inner ear; for example, words or phrases you hear inside your head. Clairaudience can include hearing the perfect song lyrics at just the right time, overhearing something in a conversation that feels important or any other way your guides get your attention through sound.

If you are clairaudient you may pull an oracle card and hear extra words or phrases being said to you, you may suddenly have song lyrics pop into your head or hear the voices of your guides speaking to you. Clairaudient guidance will always be loving, kind, supportive and helpful and will always show you the best available path. If you are hearing any voices that do not feel loving or kind it's always a good idea to seek help from a professional.

TO WAKE UP YOUR CLAIRAUDIENCE:

✦ Prepare your energy for a reading.

✦ Close your eyes and get still and quiet in meditation.

✦ Take some time to really listen to the sounds around you: creaks in the walls, sounds from other rooms or the sounds of nature outside. Notice if you hear anything with your inner ear.

✦ When you're ready, open your eyes.

✦ Record everything you heard.

TO DEVELOP YOUR CLAIRAUDIENCE:

✦ Listen to everything: bird song, the wind in the trees, music, song lyrics, spoken-word poetry, audio books, podcasts and so on.

✦ Listen to high-vibrational music while you meditate.

✦ Pick a playlist and hit shuffle, paying attention to the lyrics that come through and considering how they could be messages from your guides.

TRY THIS ORACLE PRACTICE:

✦ Pull an oracle card and ask yourself if this card had a sound, what would it be?

✦ Pull an oracle card and notice if you hear any sounds, words or phrases in your inner ear.

✦ Pull a card and assign a sound or song to it.

Pull a card!

Ask these questions:

✦ How can I wake up and activate my clairaudience?

✦ How am I already using my clairaudience?

✦ How can I continue to develop and strengthen my clairaudience?

CLAIRSENTIENCE

Clairsentience means 'clear feeling' and is all about receiving psychic messages through your emotions and the physical feelings in your body. If you're clairsentient, pulling oracle cards may activate physical sensations or emotional responses within you. Always pay attention to what's happening in your body, and when you feel strong emotions ask yourself: 'What is this emotion or physical feeling trying to tell me?'

Clairsentience usually manifests as feelings that come and then pass quickly. If something in your body doesn't feel right, while it can be a message from your guides you should always check out any unusual physical issues you're concerned about.

TO WAKE UP YOUR CLAIRSENTIENCE:

✦ Prepare your energy for a reading.

✦ Close your eyes and get still and quiet in meditation.

✦ Scan your physical body and notice how you're feeling – where you're feeling tight or sore – and consider what message your body may be giving you through this physical feeling.

✦ Pay attention to your emotional body. What emotions are you feeling right now? What do you think they are trying to tell you?

✦ When you're ready, open your eyes.

✦ Record any physical sensations or emotions and what you feel they might be telling you.

TO DEVELOP YOUR CLAIRSENTIENCE:

✦ Pay attention to your emotions and get curious about what they are trying to tell you.

✦ Listen to the wisdom of your body.

✦ Practise yoga or any other activity that gets you moving and more deeply connected with your body.

TRY THIS ORACLE PRACTICE:

✦ Pull an oracle card and notice how it makes you feel emotionally.

✦ Pull an oracle card and notice where you feel the energy of this card in your body.

✦ Pull a card and ask if this card was a physical sensation, what would it be?

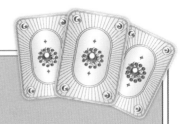

Pull a card!

Ask these questions:

✦ How can I wake up and activate my clairsentience?
✦ How am I already using my clairsentience?
✦ How can I continue to develop and strengthen my clairsentience?

CLAIRCOGNISANCE

Claircognisance means 'clear knowing', and this can often be the most difficult clair to get to grips with. Claircognisance is the guidance that comes in through thoughts or knowing, and since you think a million thoughts per second then knowing when it's guidance or when it's just your regular old monkey mind can take some practice.

You may be claircognisant if you sometimes just know something without really knowing how you know. During oracle readings, you may find that you pull a card and you just know exactly what your guides are telling you and what you need to do next.

TO WAKE UP YOUR CLAIRCOGNISANCE:

✦ Prepare your energy for a reading.
✦ Close your eyes and get still and quiet in meditation.

+ Pay attention just to your thoughts – notice when your mind wanders and where it goes – and think about your thinking. Don't judge; just notice.

+ Try to quieten your mind and bring yourself back to centre. Notice what thoughts and ideas come through now that your mind is more focused.

+ Pay extra attention to any thoughts that feel very clear or repetitive.

+ When you're ready, open your eyes.

+ Record anything and everything that feels important to remember or journal out.

TO DEVELOP YOUR CLAIRCOGNISANCE:

+ In the morning, record everything that freely flows into your head for 10 minutes to help clear your mind.

+ Pay attention to the thoughts and ideas that cut across your mind clearly or that keep repeating on you.

+ Ground your energy.

+ Work on clearing and focusing your mind.

TRY THIS ORACLE PRACTICE:

+ Pull an oracle card and quickly notice the first thing that pops into your mind.

+ Pull an oracle card and spend some time journalling or free writing everything that comes to mind. When you're done, read it through and circle the parts that feel important.

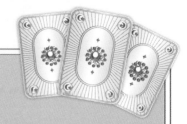

Pull a card!

Ask these questions:

+ How can I wake up and activate my claircognisance?
+ How am I already using my claircognisance?
+ How can I continue to develop and strengthen my claircognisance?

DEVELOPING THE CLAIRS

A really simple way to develop your psychic and intuitive ability using all the clairs is to immediately ask yourself these questions any time you pull a card:

+ What's the first thing you think of when you turn this card over?
+ How does this card make you feel?
+ What image on the card catches your attention?
+ Which words or phrases are you drawn to?

Is it guidance or are you making it up? To help you decide, consider the following:

✦ Divine or intuitive guidance should always feel loving and kind. If any messages you get ever feel fearful it's most likely these messages are coming from your own fears and worries and not any kind of higher guidance.

✦ Your guidance may push you out of your comfort zone but it will never advise you to do something that would cause harm to you or others.

✦ Your guidance will usually feel clearer or louder than your regular thoughts, emotions or mental visions.

✦ Ask yourself what's the worst thing that can happen if you follow this guidance, and what's the best thing that could happen.

✦ Trust yourself: if the guidance feels good, go for it! One of the biggest things that can hold you back from becoming psychic is not trusting your guidance, never acting on it or never taking a leap of faith. Sometimes you have to make a mistake and follow the wrong breadcrumbs before you can recognise the right ones.

The more you follow the guidance you get the easier it will be to hear it and trust it the next time. Soon it will just become second nature to be able to connect with your guides and your inner knowing.

DECODING YOUR CARDS

As your intuition and psychic ability grow you will develop a communication system with your guides through the cards that works for you, but while there will be times when you get the guidance you're looking for as soon as you turn over a card, sometimes you will have to dive a little deeper for the messages. When you don't get what a card is trying to tell you straight away it can be tempting to put it aside and pull another card until you get one that gives you a quick and clear answer; however, there is a whole world of information, symbolism and hidden messages available to you on each card. When you take the time to decode and decipher the messages and meaning in the card right in front of you, you'll not only get a much deeper and more involved reading but you will also be strengthening your intuition and psychic muscles.

As you go through this process of decoding the elements of an oracle card be mindful of the fact that we all have different associations with the symbols and elements based on our cultural background, belief system, personal experiences and likes and dislikes. If the meanings here don't resonate with you, honour your own. The universe speaks to you in ways you can understand, so always decode symbols and elements according to your own viewpoint. The following is just a guide to get you started. Not all of the keywords and phrases listed for each element will be relevant to your reading. Use your intuition as you decode the cards and pay attention to the meanings that feel right for you, your question and your reading.

Before you continue reading, take a moment to record in your journal some of the symbols and signs you often notice in the world around you or in your oracle card-reading practice. Make a quick note of what these symbols and signs mean to you personally.

Colours

Colour is usually one of the main features of an oracle card and can add a powerful layer to your readings. For example, the card backs for the *Goddesses Among Us* oracle are pink and yellow, which at first glance may just seem like a nice colour combination and a design choice. However, as pink represents the heart chakra, love and femininity and yellow relates to the solar plexus chakra and the colour of personal power, these card backs offer a hidden message about activating the heart and your power through the cards. Deck creators don't always have space in the guidebook to explain every single symbol but that's perfect, because it leaves it up to you to discover!

✦ **White,** ether element: peace, spirit, clear, clean, pure, simple, spiritual, bridal; the aura (expanded being).

✦ **Yellow,** fire element: happiness, optimism, hopefulness, positivity, warmth, radiance; solar plexus chakra (personal power).

✦ **Orange,** fire element: joy, enthusiasm, abundance, stimulation, enjoyment, excitement, sexuality; sacral chakra (creativity and emotions).

✦ **Red,** earth element: love, passion, lust, desire, action, confidence, war, anger, danger, energy, willpower; root chakra (material needs).

✦ **Blue,** water element: calm, trust, truth, peace, freedom, communication, imagination, expansiveness, inspiration; throat chakra (self-expression).

✦ **Green,** earth element: nature, growth, life, renewal, healing, fertility, money, finances, jealousy; heart chakra (love).

✦ **Purple,** ether element: spirituality, religion, royalty, luxury, devotion, mystery, magic; crown chakra (wisdom).

✦ **Grey,** air element: cool, neutral, conservative, athletic, emotionless, boredom, loss, depression.

✦ **Pink,** fire element: love, romance, playfulness, sweetness, kindness, friendship, childhood, inner child, femininity, acceptance; heart chakra (love).

✦ **Turquoise,** water and air elements: cool, calm, refreshing, tranquillity, patience, intuition, communication, wisdom, spirituality; throat (self-expression) and heart chakras (love).

✦ **Brown,** earth element: earthy, nature, natural, security, home, stability, warmth, dependable; earth star chakra (grounding).

✦ **Black,** earth element: magic, power, protection, the void, fear, the shadow, the unknown, authority, formality, grief, death, mourning.

✦ **Rainbow,** all encompassing, light, the collective, joy, wonder, awe, inner child, magic, possibility, LGBTQ+ community.

✦ **Silver,** ether element: clarity, reflection, wisdom, sleekness, modern, high tech, wealth, stars, space travel, eloquence, psychic abilities, meditation.

✦ **Gold,** earth element: prosperity, wealth, money, riches, power, success, illumination, high value, higher spiritual wisdom, ascension; soul star chakra (connection to the soul and higher self).

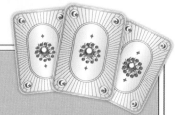

Pull a card!

Pull a few cards and decode the hidden messages of the colours used in the artwork.

Numerology and angel numbers

You can use any of the numbers that appear on your oracle cards as part of your reading. In numerology, we usually add down to a single digit. For example, if you get card number 36 you add 3 + 6 for a total of 9. You can, however, also read the numbers individually and look at the meaning of both 3 and 6 as well as or instead of adding them together.

✦ **0:** innocence, youth, beginnings, the moment before the inhale (0 is not generally used in oracle cards but in the tarot this is the number of The Fool card).

✦ **1:** manifestation, magic, individuality, decisions, independence, sovereignty, new beginnings, clean slate, the first day of the rest of your life.

✦ **2:** partnerships, deep connection, soulmates, lovers, duality, two sides of the coin, balance, harmony, alignment, peace.

✦ **3:** creativity, birth, collaboration, holy trinity, growth, expansion, teamwork.

- ✦ **4:** stability, material world, structure, maturity, leadership, hard work, order, predictability.
- ✦ **5:** change, freedom, chaos, conflict, challenge, adventure, unpredictability, unknown.
- ✦ **6:** love, beauty, flow, cooperation, balanced energy exchange, generosity, masculine/feminine alignment or yin/yang balance.
- ✦ **7:** spirituality, knowledge, wisdom, luck, magic.
- ✦ **8:** abundance, money, forward movement, transformation, eternity.
- ✦ **9:** completion, the end of a cycle, accomplishment, finishing things up, endings, wholeness.

The master numbers are 11, 22 and 33 and they do not get added down; they are considered to be very high-vibrational numbers and hold 10 times more power and energy than single digits. These numbers hold both their single digit energy as well as the number they add up to:

- ✦ **11:** a powerful manifestation number, intuitive, psychic, enlightenment, breakthrough, awakening.
- ✦ **22:** a number of deep connection with others and the divine, achievement, life purpose, dreams coming true.
- ✦ **33:** a number of success and growth, high-vibrational creativity, creating your own destiny, divine inspiration.

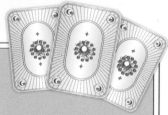

Pull a card!

Pull a few oracle cards and decode the numbers that appear.

Symbolism

Oracle deck creators include so many different symbols in their work that it would be impossible to list them all here. However, there are some common symbols that appear on oracle cards and understanding their meanings can give your readings deeper meaning. Symbols always mean different things to different people so, again, you may find it useful to consider what these symbols mean to you personally on top of the more collective meanings below.

The planets

+ **Moon:** intuition, mystery, divine feminine wisdom.

+ **Full moon:** birth, fulfilment, gratitude, releasing.

+ **New moon:** conception, new beginnings, manifestation.

+ **Moon phases**: cycles, birth, life, death, rebirth.

+ **Sun:** light, growth, power, activation, joy, optimism, divine masculine wisdom.

+ **Stars:** ascension, higher self, star beings, guides, the soul.

- **Mercury:** communication, messages, self-expression, ideas.
- **Venus:** love, values, wisdom, prosperity.
- **Earth:** environment, caring for the earth, grounding, abundance, gratitude, unity, home.
- **Mars:** war, aggression, passion, action.
- **Jupiter:** expansion, growth, luck, abundance.
- **Saturn:** structure, responsibility, maturity.
- **Uranus:** innovation, rebelliousness, discovery, technology.
- **Neptune:** dreams, illusions, subconscious, psychic receptivity.
- **Pluto:** transformation, endings and beginnings, rebirth, spiritual growth.

The elements

- **Earth:** grounding, connecting with nature, material world, money, work, finances; root and earth star chakras.
- **Water:** relationships, love, intuition, dreams, subconscious, psychic abilities; heart chakra.
- **Air/sky:** thoughts and ideas, communication, spirituality, spiritual connection, ether, spirit; crown chakra.
- **Fire:** passion, action, activism, making it happen, travel, adventure; solar plexus and sacral chakras.
- **Metal:** strength, courage, power, protection, clarity.
- **Wood:** integrity, life, growth, strength.

Shapes

✦ **Circle:** wholeness, perfection, totality, never-ending, cycles.

✦ **Spiral**: growth, expansion, consciousness, evolution, awareness.

✦ **Square:** structure, stability, balance, logic, law and order.

✦ **Triangle**: manifestation, creativity, enlightenment, revelation, higher awareness.

Spiritual symbols

✦ **Pentagram:** coming together of the elements of air, earth, fire, water and ether/spirit, Wicca, witchcraft, spells, magic, protection.

✦ **Star of David:** six directions (north, south, east, west, up and down), protection, Judaism, Kabbalah, protection, connecting heaven and earth.

✦ **Cross:** sacrifice, ascension, everlasting life, salvation, protection.

✦ **Ankh:** eternal life, wisdom, insight, protection.

✦ **Flower of life:** cycle of life, creation, interconnectedness, the collective.

✦ **Metatron's cube:** creation, nature, release of negativity, spiritual balance, knowledge.

- ✦ **Tree of life:** midpoint between heaven (leaves) and earth (roots), interconnectedness, personal and spiritual growth, nurturing, nourishment, ancestry, legacy.

- ✦ **Eye:** protection, psychic vision, clairvoyance, clarity, awareness, gateway to the soul.

- ✦ **Eye of Horus (left eye):** healing, protection, wisdom, rebirth, resurrection, good luck.

- ✦ **Eye of Ra (right eye):** power, fury, protection, royal authority, sun god.

- ✦ **Ouroboros:** eternity, the cycle of death and rebirth.

Animals

- ✦ **Butterfly:** transformation, rebirth, hope, passed-over loved ones.
- ✦ **Bird:** enlightenment, freedom, elevation, big picture, rising above, focus.
- ✦ **Snake:** the shadow, shedding, transformation, feminine power, kundalini rising, eternity.
- ✦ **Cat:** intuition, boundaries, pleasure, independence, psychic world.
- ✦ **Dog:** loyalty, trust, friendship, generosity, protection.
- ✦ **Deer:** peace, gentleness, grace, awareness, spirituality, unconditional love; heart chakra.
- ✦ **Horse:** freedom, majesty, courage, perseverance, integrity, power, faithfulness.

- ✦ **Mouse:** details, resources, motivation.
- ✦ **Insect**: community, tenacity, patience, collective, common good.
- ✦ **Spider**: fear, shadow work, weaving, connection, creativity.
- ✦ **Bee:** hard work, commitment, collective consciousness, sacred feminine, manifestation, good luck, spirit world.
- ✦ **Dragon:** fierceness, protection, clearing the path ahead, travel.
- ✦ **Unicorn:** magic, inner child, joy, purity, illumination.

Nature

- ✦ **Feather:** angels, spirit, passed-over loved ones.
- ✦ **Flower:** abundance, joy, happiness, fertility, growth.
- ✦ **Rose:** divine feminine, heart opening, love, beauty.
- ✦ **Wildflower:** wildness, freedom, expansion.
- ✦ **Tree:** grounding, strength, growth.
- ✦ **Crystal:** earth connection, higher consciousness, higher awareness.
- ✦ **Cloud:** dreams, the mind, spiritual guidance, calm, meditation.
- ✦ **Mountain:** reaching goals, pushing limits, pilgrimages, higher viewpoint, elevation.
- ✦ **Lake/ocean:** depth, subconscious, vastness, mystery, calm, peace, endlessness.
- ✦ **Fruit:** abundance, sweetness of life, joy, nourishment.

Other symbols

+ **Heart:** love, romantic love, self-love.
+ **Trinity knot:** power of three, magic, cycles.
+ **Celtic knot:** interconnection, endlessness, eternity.
+ **Key:** secrets, locking, unlocking, discovering, wisdom keeper, finding answers.
+ **Gate/portal:** transition, transformation, change, releasing, evolving, becoming, next chapter.
+ **Coin or money:** abundance, prosperity, success, work.
+ **Skull:** death, endings, afterlife, ancestors.
+ **Light:** illumination, inner light, mysteries unveiled, wisdom, guides.
+ **Vessel, cup or bowl:** divine feminine, goddess, emotions, intuition.
+ **Boat**: travel, movement, sailing away.
+ **Building**: structure, routine, grounding, physical world.
+ **Sword/dagger**: protection, power, courage, clarity.
+ **Crown:** royalty, power, sovereignty, legacy, hierarchy.
+ **Wing:** spirit, elevation, ascension, rising above.
+ **Wand:** magic, manifestation, making it happen.

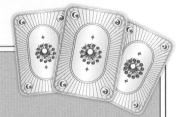

Pull a card!

Pull a few cards from your deck and identify as many symbols as you can. Find the meanings above, or if they aren't listed or don't resonate come up with your own meanings for each of the symbols you see. Record your insights in your journal.

Decoding keywords and phrases

Most oracle cards feature the name of the card: either a name of the guide represented or a simple word or two followed by some keywords or phrases. Pay attention to which words you are drawn to; it may be a particular keyword or a word in the middle of a phrase. Not all of the keywords will always be relevant to each situation, question or reading, so being able to hone in on the part of the text that is for you in the moment can help turn a general reading into something much more personal.

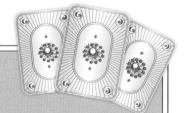

Pull a card!

Formulate a question in your mind, shuffle your deck and pull a card. Immediately notice which word or words your eyes are drawn to. The trick here is to not think about it too much but to trust you will be drawn to the word/s you need to see in this moment.

When you very quickly scan a card you are not giving your logical mind a chance to overthink; instead, you are letting your intuition lead you. Always trust what you notice first then go on to dive more deeply into the card as you need to.

Decoding practice

Prepare your space then your energy for a reading and focus your mind on a question as you shuffle your cards. Pull just one card and write down the following:

✦ What's the first part of the image you notice: colour, shape, symbol and so on?

✦ What keyword or phrase jumps out at you?

✦ What do you think this card is trying to tell you?

✦ Take some time to decode the other imagery in the card.

✦ Focus on which symbols or elements feel most important to you in this moment and help answer your question.

PATHWORKING

'Pathworking' is a word often used in tarot reading, but you can do pathworking just as easily with your oracle cards. Essentially, pathworking is a practice of imagining you are stepping into the cards on a kind of meditative journey to help you fully experience them and the messages they have for you.

If there's an angel, other figure, person or animal on the card you can visualise yourself *becoming* them and discovering how they are feeling and what they are thinking. Another method is to step into the card as yourself and sit down with the figure on the card and ask them any questions you may have. Both of these ways of pathworking work really well when using oracle cards that feature guides, spiritual beings, angels or goddesses (like the *Angels Among Us* and *Goddesses Among Us* oracle decks).

If the cards you're using feature landscapes you can journey into those landscapes. Walk around, turn around, look in all directions and explore: see where your meditation takes you. The wonderful thing about pathworking is that there really are no rules because it's all about you having your own deep experience with and in the cards.

This practice can still work when using a deck with a more abstract art style. Take yourself into the abstract world and see what you find. If you have a deck featuring different crystals, flowers or other objects you can mentally reach in and take hold of the object and feel it in your hand, breathe in and let the flower's scent speak to you or let the crystal pass on its wisdom.

This is such an intuitive and creative process, so enjoy the journey! However you feel called to step into the imagery of the card is perfect. Begin by choosing an oracle deck you think would work well for this practice, then:

✦ Prepare your space (see Chapter 1).

✦ Prepare your energy (see Chapter 1).

✦ Connect with your guides or whatever you want to connect with during this reading and journey.

✦ Set an intention to receive guidance and have a deeper experience with your oracle cards.

✦ Ask to be shown a card that would be most beneficial for you to explore more deeply today.

- ✦ Shuffle your deck and wait for a card to pop or fall out or call to you.

- ✦ Turn the card over and take a moment to look at the imagery. With your eyes open still looking at the card or with your eyes closed, visualise yourself stepping into the card.

- ✦ Take some time to look around, explore the landscape, touch or hold any objects or communicate with any beings present.

- ✦ Allow yourself to fully immerse yourself, noticing the sounds and scents around you, how the air feels on your skin and how the ground feels beneath your feet.

- ✦ While you are in the meditation you can ask questions and stay open to even more guidance coming through.

- ✦ When you feel you've received everything you can from the experience, thank any beings or energies who were present with you and step back out of the card.

- ✦ Take some moments to record any insights in your journal.

- ✦ This can be deeply spiritual work, so take a moment to ground your energy again (see Chapter 1) when you are done.

REVERSALS

A 'reversed' card is one that appears upside down in your reading. Reading oracle cards with reversals is completely optional, but it can be useful if you want to add another layer of information to your readings. To shuffle your deck for reversals you can:

- Hold the deck in your non-dominant hand, and with your dominant hand begin to swirl or spin the deck so that the cards end up in all directions.
- Place the deck on a table: cut the deck in half, turn it around then place it back on the top of the deck and shuffle as usual.
- Spread the deck out on the floor or a large table and smoosh the cards in all directions before combining them back into a single deck.

When a card comes up reversed in your readings you can view it in a number of different ways:

- The energy may be stuck or blocked. For example, if you pull a card on love or romance and it's reversed it may suggest you have a block in this area and may not be letting love in. The message could be about working on releasing this block so you can be open to the love coming into your life.
- Read the card as the opposite. For example, if you pull a card of prosperity reversed it could suggest you are in a mindset of lack. To keep your readings empowering, remember that *you* always have the power to turn things around. Whatever you are experiencing can be shifted and changed!
- Look at reversed cards as showing you your potential. You may not yet be fully aligned with the energy of the card but the card is still there in your reading. It's still a possibility, something you *can* achieve and experience; you may just have to take some extra steps to fully realise it.

- Reversed cards can show you what you're not paying attention to, something you are ignoring or that is hidden deep in your subconscious but wants to come to the surface to be looked at.

- Reversed cards can also be an opportunity for shadow work (which we will talk about more in Chapter 4). Reversed cards can show us what we are afraid of, what aspects of ourselves we are unwilling to accept or work on or things we don't want others to see.

Reading with reversals can still be wonderfully empowering as long as you feel ready to really do the work and don't mind your guides showing you places where there is opportunity for change, learning and growth.

REPEATING CARDS

Sometimes referred to as 'stalker' cards, although that's slightly problematic for obvious reasons, these cards never seem to leave you alone. No matter whether you are doing one-card readings or bigger spreads, they always seem to show up.

It can be tempting to think maybe you haven't shuffled properly, and sometimes that's true. If you've just pulled a card and put it back in the deck and don't shuffle well that card can be more likely to come up again as it may still be poking out of the deck slightly. When you've shuffled for a while and these cards still appear you may start to feel like there is a deeper reason for this, and usually there is.

It can feel annoying to see the same cards all the time, especially if they aren't the cards you really want to see, but understanding why they are coming up so often is the first step in changing the pattern. These may be some of the reasons you see repeating cards:

✦ This may where you're vibrating energetically. The cards often mirror where you are energetically, so if you keep pulling the same card – the same angel, chakra or crystal – it may just be that this is where you're at right now or what you need to keep focusing on working through.

✦ You're not paying attention to the advice the card is giving you. If you keep pulling that boundaries card but do absolutely nothing to create better boundaries with people then nothing is going to change and you're probably going to keep getting the same advice until you start making those changes.

✦ Sometimes it takes a long time to process, work through and learn a lesson. There is no shame at all in seeing the same card over and over for months at a time as long as you're paying attention and trying to do something to move forward. Many card readers experience years of seeing the same cards over and over, and then once the lesson is learned they never see that card again!

Pull a card!

Ask these questions:

+ Why do I keep seeing this card?
+ What am I missing?
+ What is the lesson here?
+ What do I need to do so this card stops showing up?

You can do this any time you're doing a reading and one of the repeating cards shows up for you again.

Usually, when you've moved through the lesson or shifted your vibration repeating cards will stop showing up. When you start seeing cards in a deck that you've never pulled before it's time for celebration, because it means you've learned your lesson and are ready for the next one!

FINISHING A READING

At the end of your reading always take time to say 'Thank you' to your guides, angels, higher self and anyone else you feel has supported you in the reading. Taking a moment for gratitude and thanks can really help build the relationship between you and your guides.

It's often useful to take some time to just sit and meditate after a reading. Perhaps you could record your thoughts in your journal or just relax so you can let the guidance integrate or let any other guidance and wisdom come through.

Put your cards and reading cloth away to symbolise that the reading has been completed.

TROUBLESHOOTING

Are you having trouble getting the guidance you want? Here are some simple tips to try when your readings just don't seem to be making sense.

▶ **Your energy may not be centred, grounded or clear.** Revisit Chapter 1 for more information on how to do this. Also, remember that it can take time and practice to start feeling really grounded, clear and focused, so keep at it. Practise preparing your energy and doing a one-card reading for yourself every day for at least a month and you should start to notice the difference in how much more you get from your readings.

▶ **Consider the questions you're asking.** Avoid 'Should I . . .' questions. Your guides don't want to tell you how to live your life; they just want to offer you guidance, which you are always welcome to take or leave. Get clear with your questions and ask one thing at a time. Remember that the clearer the question the clearer will be the answer.

▶ **Make sure you know who or what you're communicating with through the cards.** Be clear in calling on your guides before you do a reading. If you've been asking a particular guide or energy and nothing is coming through, try connecting with someone or something else and see if that helps.

▶ **Check back in with your intention.** Why are you working with oracle cards? How do you want this practice to elevate, transform and help you grow?

▶ **Consider whether or not you're resonating with the deck you're using.** Maybe you don't really like the art style on your deck or can't connect with the keywords. Try using a different deck that you feel more drawn to.

▶ **Check in with your emotional state.** Reading when you're angry, frustrated, upset or overly emotional usually doesn't provide the clearest readings. Give yourself time and space to sense your feelings and then try again later when you are more balanced.

▶ **Ask yourself if you trust the guidance that is coming through.** People often discard their readings because they just don't believe it's really their guidance, but what if it is? Learning to trust your guidance is a process: it may not happen overnight but it will happen if you keep practising and developing your intuition. Ask yourself whether you're not getting the guidance or if you're just not *trusting* the guidance you are getting.

▶ **Here's a kicker, but perhaps you're just not getting the guidance you wanted.** So often we ask a question and already know what we want the answer to be, and when we don't get that answer we think there's something wrong with our readings when, really, it's just that we don't like the answer we've been given. If you've been getting guidance you don't like try pulling another card and asking a question such as 'How can I navigate through this?' or 'How I can learn this lesson and move on?'

▶ **Your expectations may be too big.** While there will definitely be times when your oracle-card readings completely blow you away, most of the time readings offer you subtle, gentle nudges or reminders. Be okay with the guidance that is coming through in whatever way it comes, and remember that those gentle nudges are sometimes exactly what you need to get you on your best and highest path.

NOTES

NOTES

ADVANCING YOUR PRACTICE

In this chapter we will look at how to take your oracle-card reading to the next level and how to really start making magic with your cards.

DAILY READING

Consistency is everything when it comes to advancing your oracle card reading practice. Pulling a card for yourself every day may seem like a big ask, but when you set an intention to show up and then actually do show up something very powerful happens.

People often say they don't have time for a spiritual practice, but if you really want to experience deep transformation and a more ease-filled, divinely connected life you can't afford *not* to find the time. Everyone can find at least a few minutes every day to check in with themselves if they really want to do it. Setting the alarm for 5 minutes earlier in the morning or going to bed 5 minutes later isn't going to change your entire day that much, but it could change your whole life if you use those 5 minutes to connect with your guides and inner guidance.

A spiritual practice can be as short and simple or long and involved as you have the time and space for. Even if you just dedicate 1 minute a day to pulling a card you'll soon become more intuitive and connected in every other moment of your day. Here are some examples of a short daily practice:

✦ Keep an oracle deck on your bedside table. As soon as you wake up, reach over and pull a card for the day. Take a few moments to meditate on the message and set an intention for the day ahead.

+ Before going to sleep, pull a card for yourself and journal a few words or paragraphs on what comes up for you.

+ Carry a deck with you and pull a card in your car, during your commute, on a break or, if you absolutely have no other choice and no other time, pulling a card in a bathroom stall is nothing to be ashamed of. We've all done it!

+ Put your deck next to the kettle, and while you're waiting for the kettle to boil for your morning tea or coffee, ask the question that's most in your heart and pull yourself a card.

Slightly longer practices could include the following:

+ In your sacred space, prepare your energy for a reading: clearing, protecting and grounding your energy. Set your intention and ask your question or what you need to know about the day ahead and pull a card. Record a few notes in your journal.

+ Focus on a clair you are working on developing. Prepare your energy for a reading and then set an intention to be open to receiving guidance through that clair. Shuffle the deck then pick a card and turn it over, noticing what immediately comes through. How do you feel? What do you see? What do you hear or which words stand out? Do you have a sense of just *knowing* what the card is trying to tell you? Quickly record anything that comes through the clair you're working on or any other insights.

When you have some extra time or want a longer practice you can:

✦ Set up your sacred space, prepare your energy and set your intention. Call in your guides and whatever else supports you with your readings. Choose a spread, then shuffle and pull your cards. Take some time to journal on each card pulled. When you're done, meditate on the reading and be open to any other guidance coming through.

✦ Do the same as in the previous point but pull just one card and practise pathworking (see Chapter 3). Go into the card and fully experience the energy and messages available to you.

✦ Do the same as in the first point but pull just one card and go through the process of decoding the card (see Chapter 3). Go as deep as you can with the symbolism on the card and write down everything you notice, then take some time to meditate on the card and the messages coming through for you.

✦ Again, start with the process in the first point but then work with some oracle magic or oracle healing (more about this later in this chapter).

COMBINING OTHER TOOLS
WITH CARD READINGS

Using other spiritual tools together with your oracle cards can bring more magic and clarity to your readings and enhance them.

TO WORK WITH CRYSTALS:

✦ Hold a clear quartz crystal while reading to help you form a direct connection with your guidance and get a clearer reading.

✦ If you're struggling to ground yourself hold or carry smoky quartz, black onyx or black tourmaline during readings.

✦ To boost your intuition and connection with your guides, carry or wear amethyst when doing readings.

✦ To help open your third eye work with labradorite or any other dark blue stones. You can even place one on your third eye for a few moments before you begin.

✦ To connect with your angels during readings, hold or wear angelite or celestite.

✦ To keep your energy and space clear and cleansed, place selenite around your room or space or on your altar or wear or hold it when doing readings.

✦ For more loving and compassionate readings carry or wear rose quartz.

✦ You can hold, wear or have any other crystals you're drawn to in your reading space to help amplify your intention, clarity and/or connection.

WORK WITH OILS IN THE FOLLOWING WAYS:

✦ frankincense for intuition, spiritual connection and sacred space

✦ lavender for sacred space, calming and relaxation

✦ palo santo for sacred space, clearing and cleansing

✦ sage for clearing and cleansing

✦ sandalwood for meditation and connection with your guides

✦ rosemary for cleansing and protection

✦ lemon for energy, focus and elevation

✦ rose for love, compassion and heart opening.

TO USE YOUR OILS:

✦ Place them in an oil burner or diffuser to create clear and sacred space.

✦ Anoint your wrists and heart with a diluted oil.

✦ Put drops of an oil onto your hands (check it is safe to use directly on skin and, if not, dilute it) and rub them together. Once the oil has begun to sink into your skin shuffle your cards, which will infuse the oil into your deck. Be careful not to put too much oil on your hands as you may damage the deck.

✦ Anoint the edges of your cards with light dabs of oil to align them with your intention for readings.

WORK WITH INCENSE IN THE FOLLOWING WAYS:

✦ Light a herb bundle, stick of palo santo or incense stick and waft it around your space, over your altar or around yourself to clear any negativity before you begin a reading.

✦ Waft the smoke around your deck to clear its energy before reading.

✦ Light a stick of frankincense incense during readings to keep the vibration high and the space sacred.

YOU CAN ALSO TRY ANY OF THESE OTHER TOOLS:

✦ Having a special candle you use when you are doing readings can be a great way to set the intention you are about to read to symbolise bringing light to the situation and/or to honour whoever is bringing the guidance through for you.

✦ Use sound healing tools such as tingshas, singing bowls, crystal bowls or bells to clear the space, clear yourself and clear your cards before and after reading.

✦ Aura sprays can be used to clear you and your space and create a sacred space before a reading.

✦ You may like to dedicate a specific piece of jewellery to your oracle-card reading practice. Set an intention that whenever you wear it your readings will be clear, empowering and helpful for you on your path.

Using both tarot and oracle cards in a reading can add a powerful extra layer of guidance. Tarot is often more concerned with the nitty gritty of life (especially the minor arcana), while oracle cards can offer you a more straightforward, spiritual and often bigger picture viewpoint. Using them together can help you see both the details and the higher perspective. To combine tarot and oracle cards in a reading:

✦ Pull one tarot card and one oracle card for each card position of a spread.

✦ Do your main spread with the deck and place one to three oracle cards around the spread for extra guidance.

✦ Pull an oracle card as an overview or theme of the reading and then pull tarot cards to give you the details.

✦ Pull an oracle card to show you the higher purpose or the big why of what's going on in your tarot reading.

✦ If you are working with a deck that features guides or spiritual beings, pull one to three cards to show you who is working with you at this time or who to call on for help with whatever is going on in your tarot reading.

✦ Do a reading using just oracle cards and use the tarot as clarifying cards if you need more information or if more questions come up for you.

✦ Pull one oracle card for guidance then pull one tarot card as an action step on how to move forward with that guidance.

Get creative and find some other ways to work with both tarot and oracle cards that work for you!

> *Important note*: if you don't have the tools listed above you don't have to run out to buy something new, as magic is more about intention than having the right thing. Using what you have is what magical folk have been doing for centuries. When buying something new, always look for ethically sourced palo santo, sage, crystals, oils and incense, because purchasing ethically always makes a big difference to the energy of your tools and your practice.

MANIFESTATION

Manifestation essentially is making something real. When you work with any magical practices including oracle magic you become more intentional and clearer about what you want, move into deeper alignment with your desires and discover what action you need to take to meet the universe halfway and make it happen.

Before you start working with any manifestation practices, take some time to tune in to your oracle cards and work out what it is you really want and need in your life.

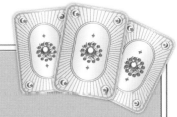

Pull a card!

Pull some cards and ask these questions:

✦ What does my heart and soul most want to manifest?

✦ Is there anything blocking this?

✦ How can I clear this block?

✦ How can I make this happen?

The following manifestation practices all involve using your cards as visual prompts to remind you what it is you are manifesting. When you use the cards in this way it will help you stay focused on what you want, remind you when you are going off course with your own thoughts, beliefs or actions and also bring the energy of what you want into your space and life.

✦ Set up a manifestation altar: this could be a coffee table, shelf or even your bedside table. If you like you can place any magical tools, statues, candles or crystals on your altar that symbolise what you want manifested. Choose an oracle card that represents what you want to manifest and place that card on your altar, leaving it there until it has manifested or until you want to manifest something new.

- If you don't have an altar, take the card that symbolises what you want to call into your life and place it somewhere you will see it often. If you're trying to call in a new job, for example, you might place the card on your desk, and if you're trying to call in a new lover then place the card next to your bed.

- Take a photo of a card that symbolises what you want to manifest and make it the lock screen on your phone. This is such a simple way to manifest but one of the most effective, as you will see it often and take it with you everywhere.

Here are some really empowering and fun ways to use your oracle cards to manifest through your readings.

- Begin by doing a regular three-card reading for yourself using the positions of past, present and potential future (see Chapter 5 for this and other spreads). Shuffle your deck and pull the first two cards as you usually would, taking on the advice and guidance offered. Now, instead of shuffling for the final card, choose it upright from the deck. Where do you want to go from here and what would you like your potential future to be? Place that card in the potential future position. Record this reading in your journal and take a photo of the cards. Leave the spread on your altar for a few days or longer. Know that you have chosen your outcome and start working towards it.

- Do a three-card reading for yourself but choose all three cards upright. Choose one card to represent where you've been, one to represent where you are now and one to show where you're going next. Record this reading in your journal and take a photo or leave the card out to help you remember where you're going next.

✦ Use any spread of your choosing, but instead of shuffling for the cards consciously choose them upright from the deck and place them down. You can choose all of the cards upright or pull a mixture of cards face down and face up depending on in which area you want guidance and how you want to decide what happens.

✦ Work with any spread as you usually would, shuffling and asking for guidance. Once you've turned the cards over and if you see any cards you don't like, swap them for cards that feel better. Be aware not to use this as a way to avoid the work or bypass what's really going on but to consciously choose something better for yourself moving forward and then make it happen!

✦ Use your oracle cards to write your own story. Choose as many cards as you like to represent where you've been, where you are now and where you want things to go from here. See these cards as a plot summary of your life and record the story in your journal as if it's all already happened.

Working with affirmations is a highly effective way to reprogram any thoughts and beliefs that may be holding you back from manifesting your dream life.

Pull a card!

Ask these questions:

✦ What thoughts and beliefs are blocking my ability to manifest what I want?

✦ What do I most need to affirm for myself right now to help shift these blocks?

Take the message of your card and turn it into an affirmation. For example, if you pull a card around abundance you may like to affirm by saying *'I am abundant and I always have an overflowing supply of everything I need.'* Write your affirmation on a sticky note and place it somewhere you'll see it every day: on your altar, lock screen or bathroom mirror. Say the affirmation – out loud is best – followed by *'And so it is'* at least three times every day.

Whenever you need inspiration for a new affirmation to work with, check in with your oracle deck.

A well-known way to manifest what you want is through visualisation, and just like we did in the pathworking section in the previous chapter you can also use oracle cards to help you visualise what you want by following these steps:

✦ Choose a card that represents what it is you want to manifest.

✦ Prepare your energy for a reading and get into a deeply relaxed state.

- Take yourself into the card by visualising yourself stepping into the card.
- Notice how you feel and begin to fully experience the energy and the outcome you want for yourself.
- Take some time to explore, really feeling the thing you want in your hands or in your experience and noticing any smells and the air on your skin. Listen to the sounds around you and really feel what you want as if it's happening to you now.
- As you gently step back out of the card, don't lose that memory of how it felt to have everything you wanted.
- Do this practice as many times as you like to help you visualise and manifest your dream life!

MAGICAL WORKINGS

The possibilities for how to work with oracle cards in magic and spellwork really are unlimited. As you work with magic in your practices, always ask that the outcome be in alignment with your best and highest good. This is like a fail-safe that means you may not always get what you want but you'll always get the highest outcome.

Simple magic

Some of the practices in this section involve carrying cards with you or putting them in unusual places, so you may like to have a deck that you dedicate to simple magic. Buy a second copy of your favourite oracle deck to do these activities with or just get comfortable with having a very well-used and dog-eared deck!

✦ Place an oracle card that symbolises protection next to or over the front door of your house or on the dashboard of your car.

✦ Carry an oracle card with you that represents confidence, courage, protection, success or anything else you want to be aligned with during the day. This practice is great if you have a big work meeting or interview!

✦ Place a card under your pillow or next to your bed to help you dream of what you want, keep nightmares at bay, for protection in the dream space or for night-time manifestation or restful sleep.

✦ Place a card that represents focus, creativity or success on your desk or stick it to your computer.

✦ Infuse water, oils or any other magical items by placing them on top of a card that symbolises what you want to activate the item with.

✦ Carry a card that represents prosperity in your purse or wallet.

✦ When going on a date, carry a card with you that represents positive loving relationships.

✦ Clear, charge and activate your crystals by placing them on top of cards that align with the energies you want those crystals to be attuned to.

✦ Give single oracle cards as gifts to strengthen your relationships.

Oracle candle spell

Adding some oracle magic to your candle spells can give you extra focus and intention and a big boost to the magic you are working with. The following is just a basic guideline, so feel free to make it your own:

✦ Gather together your supplies. You will need your oracle cards; a candle (white works best for any spell or you can choose a colour that matches your intention such as pink for love, gold for success and green for healing or money); something sharp to carve into your candle such as a crystal point, pin or earring back; an oil that matches your intention (see earlier in this chapter for more information on how to use oils); a candleholder; and matches or a lighter.

✦ Clear and set up your sacred space.

✦ Prepare your energy by clearing, grounding and protecting the space and yourself.

✦ Call in your guides, which you can do by saying: *'Thank you, guides, for being with me, guiding me and supporting me in this spellwork today.'*

✦ Set an intention and say out loud or to yourself what is the spell you want to cast. For example, you can say: *'I'm here at my altar today to cast a spell for* [what you want].*'*

✦ Go through your oracle deck and choose a card or two that represent what it is you want to bring into your life. With each candle spell just focus on one thing; for example, if you're calling in love you may use cards that symbolise love such as roses, rose quartz, partnerships and archangels or goddesses associated with love. If you want to do a spell for money as well it would be better to work another spell for that.

✦ Place your card in front of the candle or put one card on either side of the candle.

✦ Take a moment to meditate on these cards and your intention, getting really clear in your mind and in your heart about what you want.

✦ Hold the candle at your heart and say out loud or in your mind a few words about what you want this candle spell to do; for example: '*I now call in* [a detailed description of what you want].'

✦ Use the pointy object to engrave a few words or symbols into the candle that represent your intention.

✦ Rub some oil into the candle while you keep focusing on your intention. A general rule here is that if you want to call something in you rub the oil down from the top to the bottom of the candle, and if you want to release something you rub the oil from the bottom to the top.

✦ Place the candle in a candle holder, light it and say: '*May this spell be cast under the law of grace, may it harm none and may the outcome be in alignment with my best and highest good.*'

✦ End your spell by saying '*And so it is*' or '*Mote it be*' three times.

✦ Thank your guides and anyone else you called in or felt was with you.

- Let the candle burn down to the bottom. If you need to pause the candle spell, use a snuffer to put out the candle and relight it when you can.

- Dispose of the candle remains. If your spell was to bring something into your life you can bury the remains in the backyard or pop them in a bin, but if your spell was to release something from your life it's best to put the remains in an outside bin or dispose of them safely somewhere away from your home.

Crystal grids

Creating a crystal grid is similar to a spell in many ways except that it uses the power of crystals to amplify energy. There are many ways to do this, and the best way – as always – is to use your intuition and intention. When setting up a crystal grid it is best to have a space where the crystals can sit undisturbed for at least a few days. Avoid doing this work on the floor or in communal areas where it may get touched or knocked.

Here is an example of one way to work with a crystal grid:

- Gather together your supplies. You will need: your oracle deck; a crystal grid mat if you have one (this is optional); and a selection of crystals – a minimum of five works best.

- Prepare your space and your energy.

- Choose an oracle card that symbolises what you would like to call in and place it on the grid mat in the centre of your altar, table or the space you are using.

- ✦ Place a crystal that also represents your intention over the card (see earlier in this chapter for more information about crystals and their associations).

- ✦ Place your crystals around the card. If you have four crystals you can place one on each side of the card. If you have more, get creative and trust your intuition for where to place them but do try to make sure your grid is equal on all sides. As you do this, hold your focus and intention on what it is you want.

- ✦ When all your crystals are set in place, hold your hand or a crystal point over the crystal in the centre. Move your hand over each of the crystals in the grid to connect them all energetically: for example, from the centre to the top, back to the centre and to the left, back to centre to the right and so on. Connect the next layer of crystals until all the crystals have been connected. There's no real rule here except to make sure you've created an energetic grid in which all of the crystals are connected with each other in some way.

- ✦ Visualise the crystal grid lit up and activated. You may like to say: '*This crystal grid is now activated and will draw in* [whatever you want to draw in]. S*o it is, and so it is and so it is.'*

- ✦ Thank your guides, the crystals and the earth element and ask that the outcome from this work be in alignment with your best and highest good.

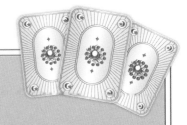

Pull a card!

Ask these questions:

+ How can I fully own my magic power?
+ How can I bring more magic into my life?
+ How can I develop my magical talents?
+ How can I use magic to get what I need and want?

ORACLE HEALING

Although oracle cards are simply a tool, they really do contain energy. Oracle-deck creators infuse their work with a great deal of love and good intentions and are often channelling higher frequencies, guidance and beings as they work. The cards themselves become a portal to the higher realms, higher beings and high-vibrational spiritual energy.

Energy healing

You can work with oracle cards for energy healing in much the same way you would if you were working with crystals or other tools. Here are some ways to explore and experience energy healing using your oracle cards:

+ Hold your hand over the card and visualise the energy of the card moving into your hand and into you. This works well for things such as confidence, abundance and peace or anything else you want to bring into your energy fields.

✦ Place any kind of love- or heart-opening card over your heart and breathe in deeply a few times, letting its energy activate your heart chakra. You can hold a card over any other chakra you would like activated.

✦ Lie down and do a full chakra balancing for yourself by placing cards that represent the chakras or chakra colours over each of your chakras. For example, place a violet, purple or crown chakra card above your head, a heart chakra card or pink card on your heart and so on. You can also do this with angels or other divine beings represented on your cards and let them heal you.

✦ To cut energetic cords or clear your energy, take a card that represents energy clearing and slice it through your aura and any negative cords of attachment.

✦ When you have a busy mind, take a card of clarity or alignment and place it above your head. Breathe deeply for a few moments.

✦ If you have any injury or illness, find a card that represents healing and place it on the part of your body that needs healing. Note that this should be done in conjunction with professional medical advice as required.

✦ To activate and open your third eye, take a third-eye or clairvoyance card and place it over your third eye while lying down. Visualise the energy healing your third eye and opening it up safely. Do this before your card readings for an extra third-eye boost!

+ To access angelic healing or healing from a higher being, choose a card or cards that represent that energy. Lie down and place the card at your heart or crown or even just beside you. Visualise the being or beings sitting with you and sending you spiritual and energetic healing.

Emotional healing

While there are times to go deep into self and spiritual development work there are also times when you just need to receive some loving, kind and gentle guidance. Oracle cards can be a comforting companion in these times, so consider these practices:

+ Choose your decks carefully, looking for ones that feel very loving, safe and supportive.
+ If it doesn't feel right asking the cards big questions, instead just ask for a supportive message to help you at this time.
+ Work with angel oracle cards as they are usually very supportive in difficult times.
+ Release the idea that you have to do anything or take any action. Sometimes it's okay to just receive a message and let it sit in your heart for a while.
+ Ask a supportive and kind friend to pull a card for you.
+ Reach out to a professional reader who you know could hold the space for your healing and let them read for you instead.
+ Let go of any pressure to even use the cards if you don't feel like it. Your cards will still be there tomorrow and the next day.

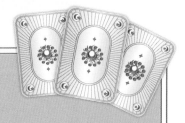

Pull a card!

Ask these questions:

✦ What needs healing?
✦ How can energy healing support me in my life right now?
✦ What can support me on my healing journey?

SHADOW WORK

The 'shadow self' is a term coined by psychologist Carl Jung, who was referencing the dark sides of people or the parts they don't want to identify with. That meaning is now often expanded to include anything and everything about ourselves or our lives we push down, ignore, disown or find challenging to look at. Shadow work can include looking at:

✦ the shadow or dark side of yourself
✦ your ego
✦ what you dislike or hide about yourself
✦ fears
✦ regrets
✦ any suffering, pain or trauma.

Shadow work can be a gentle process of healing, shedding, releasing and coming home to yourself or it can be difficult and painful, especially if you're not ready or willing to face what may come up. If you're dealing with something particularly difficult in your life – for example, any kind of deep trauma – do take care of yourself and work with a professional who can support you through the process.

It's usually best to attempt shadow work only when you feel you have good mental well-being, feel ready to work through the hard stuff and experience the growing pains and recognise what can often be uncomfortable truths. Having said all of that, if you're on a path towards a deeper connection with self or to higher levels of consciousness then bypassing shadow work can eventually cause its own problems.

Wherever you are on your journey, take it as fast or as slow as you feel you need to and trust yourself. Always avoid any practices that don't feel right or safe for you.

The most loving way is always the best way through anything on a spiritual or personal development journey. As you explore the darker places and parts of yourself, remember not to blame yourself for what comes up and instead just stay curious. There are so many reasons that we are how we are. We are essentially the product of our upbringing, cultural and media programming and of all the good and bad things that have happened to us, and it's only when we get into spiritual development that we start to realise we can take our power back. We may not be able to change the past or the things we've done, but we can choose who we want to be and how we want to move forward.

This is a lifelong journey. We are constantly working on ourselves, meeting our shadow, facing our fears and peeling away the layers of hurt as we embrace healing. Ultimately, shadow work is a process of healing, so always bear this in mind and remember to love yourself through it. No matter what you've done or what has happened to you, don't blame yourself. Just choose to step forward with love for yourself, your life and others as much as you can.

Shadow work can be about:

✦ **acceptance:** accepting the shadow aspects and letting them be
✦ **integration:** embracing, allowing and owning the shadow and letting it become part of you
✦ **transformation:** loving the shadow then letting go and making changes.

Pull a card!

Ask these questions:

✦ What aspects of my shadow do I need to love and accept?
✦ What aspects of my shadow do I need to integrate and own?
✦ What aspects of my shadow do I need to transform and change?

Shadow work in oracle reading

When you work with a guidance system such as oracle cards there are going to be times when the messages you receive shine a light on your shadow. Being prepared for it when it happens means that you are much more likely to be able to use the messages that come through to help you on your path forward instead of throwing the cards across the room and never using them again.

You won't always like what you see in your readings, and sometimes the guidance you get points to something you don't want to deal with. Maybe you asked about love and your reading showed you that you first have to heal yourself from a past relationship. Perhaps you asked about money and the message was that more money won't come until you start paying your bills on time.

It's okay to be frustrated by the guidance you get, as everyone who's ever worked with a divination system has felt like that at some point! The most powerful transformation often comes with a little discomfort. When you don't like what you see in a reading, journal on these questions:

✦ How did receiving this guidance make you feel?

✦ What did you want the messages to say?

✦ How has your ego reacted this?

✦ How has your heart reacted to this?

✦ Can you see that although this may not be what you wanted to hear it may be what you *needed* to hear?

✦ What would be the best course of action to take from here?

Your ego

When the cards don't tell you what you want to hear it's often because your ego has gotten a little prickly. 'Ego' is a difficult thing to define and is often referred to as the part of people that is focused on the self and the physical. It's the part that would take the last biscuit (even though you've already had your share) without asking if anyone else wanted it. While you do need your ego in order to navigate a physical existence, its job is essentially just to help you survive no matter what even if that means someone else has to go without. After all, if you never took any biscuits you'd soon end up pretty hungry, but your ego sometimes needs a reminder that there are enough biscuits to go around.

In another example biscuits are swapped for money, land, power and control and we are faced with the problems we see on our planet today: a society in which people are more concerned with personal gain than with how it impacts the whole. We know only too well how it plays out when world leaders have too much ego. We've all been a little too in our own ego at times, but if we don't embrace our egos at all we can find ourselves missing out on what's rightfully ours.

The flip side to living an ego-driven life is to live a heart-centred life with a little ego when required. The idea isn't to deny your ego but to understand how it's trying to help you and then use that information combined with your intuition, heart and higher guidance to help you move forward.

JOURNAL AND/OR PULL SOME CARDS ON THE FOLLOWING:

✦ What does your ego want?

✦ What does your ego want you to know?

✦ How is your ego supporting you?

✦ How is your ego hindering you?

✦ Where does your ego need to take a step back?

✦ How can you find peace and harmony with your ego?

✦ How can you share the biscuits and live from the heart?

Fear

Sometimes during oracle-card readings we'll be invited to face our fears. This can be tough as most of the time we're used to ignoring our fears, trying not to think about them or silently obsessing over them while telling everyone else that we're fine. However, when our fears come out of the shadows and into the light we usually find they aren't so scary after all, and it's a powerful opportunity to meet with them and ask them what they want to tell us. One way to do this is to think of your fears as nothing more than a scared inner child. When that scared child comes to you, take them by the hand, sit them down with a cup of hot cocoa and ask them what they are afraid of.

Our fears – in fact, all aspects of our shadow – really just want to be loved. Love is the greatest healer of all, and when we can show our fears some love they usually melt right in our arms. Having fears is a part of life. We all fear something whether it's spiders, snakes, losing a loved one or our own death. The more we bring these things out into the open and talk about them the less scary they become.

JOURNAL AND/OR PULL SOME CARDS ON THE FOLLOWING:

✦ Where does your fear come from?

✦ How is this fear trying to help you?

✦ What is this fear trying to teach you?

✦ How can you stop being so afraid of this?

✦ How can you accept, integrate or transform this fear?

✦ How can you love and let go of this fear?

Suffering

Our automatic reaction to the question 'How are you?' is usually to answer that we are fine even if the world is falling apart around us. We push our pain and suffering down so we don't have to feel it. The invitation here is to explore your pain and suffering in whatever way feels safe for you to do, although you may want to work with a trained professional on this if you've been going through something especially traumatic.

Shadow work is not about reliving your suffering but rather bringing the pain up to the surface to be seen, felt and healed. Many of us don't process emotional pain at the time it happens because it's too much to bear. We numb ourselves with alcohol, drugs, busyness and work or whatever we can do to prevent us having time to think about it. Sometimes that's exactly what we have to do in order to get through the day but eventually, one way or another, the pain from the past usually catches up with us and it's much better to decide for ourselves when that will be.

JOURNAL OR PULL SOME CARDS ON THE FOLLOWING:

✦ What old pain or suffering are you still holding on to?

✦ Why are you holding this?

✦ How is it affecting you?

✦ What would it be like to let it go?

✦ How can you let go?

✦ How can you heal?

✦ Is there any other pain or suffering you need to release?

Responsibility

Shadow work often involves looking at the parts of yourself you don't like. While oftentimes you will be much too hard on yourself and need to cut yourself a break, there will also be times when you need to take a good hard look in the mirror and make some changes.

JOURNAL AND/OR PULL SOME CARDS ON THE FOLLOWING:

✦ What aspects of yourself/ego/personality aren't working for you? You could pull a few cards to answer this question if you like.

✦ How can you make positive changes within yourself?

✦ How can you make positive changes in your life?

✦ How could making these changes help you?

✦ How could making these changes help you have a more positive impact on the world?

LIGHTWORK

'Lightwork' is a word generally used to describe any kind of spiritual or energy work that positively affects the world around you. Many people on the spiritual path feel that part of their purpose is to help humanity and the world and themselves in the process. Lightwork is all about releasing the negative aspects of your ego as much as is possible and practical and living a heart-led, compassionate life of service to love.

Lightwork isn't the flipside of shadow work; in fact, in many ways doing shadow work *is* lightwork. You can't make positive changes out in the world if you're not also facing your fears and doing your inner work, but lightwork is also about opening up to really *see* how incredible you are, to see the light in yourself and in others.

The messages you get from your oracle cards can push you out of your comfort zone for all sorts of reasons, but one of the biggest things you may struggle with is seeing your greatness, divinity and bright, shining light reflected back to you through the cards. It's not uncommon for these things to come up during shadow work, as the tendency for most of us is to blend in and dim our light. Many people disown the lightest, brightest, most incredibly amazing things about themselves and disown their power, magic and potential. However, when you do this you also shut down your ability to be of service to the divine, to love and to your heart.

When your guides show you through your oracle readings how wonderful you are, when they show you how they see you, when they show you your greatness and your potential and your true inner light, try to accept those messages. You are greater than you can possibly know. Own it, accept it and integrate it.

If you've gotten this far into this work you're here to not only change your own life for the better but also to change the world around you in ways you'll never even know about.

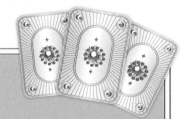

Pull a card!

Ask these questions:

✦ Where am I dimming my light?

✦ How can I activate the light within me?

✦ How can I best light up the places, people and situations closest to me?

✦ How can I be of service to love?

✦ How can I live from the heart?

✦ How am I being called to light up the world?

ORACLE MEDIUMSHIP

Using oracle cards to connect with passed-over loved ones has the potential to bring some peace and comfort. You don't need to be a trained medium to do this; all you need to do is prepare your energy for a reading, take a moment to ask whoever you'd like to connect with in spirit if they have a message for you and then pull a card and receive your message. Here are some things to consider before using your cards to contact those who have passed over:

✦ Ensure you are ready and feel safe to speak with the dead without someone more experienced being with you.

✦ Always make sure you begin a reading by preparing your space and energy.

- ✦ Be very clear about who it is you would like to call in. The best people in spirit to call in are the people who loved you and were very close to you in life and those you had positive relationships with.

- ✦ Be aware that the person you want to reach may not be available. You can always try the reading later or speak with your guides, angels or whoever else is available instead.

- ✦ Sometimes you may find the person you want to reach can only be connected with through your guides, which is still a powerful way to connect with your passed-over loved ones.

- ✦ Remember that your passed-over loved ones don't all become angels on the other side. Only call on those you know were loving in life and who would be open to connecting with you this way.

- ✦ Let go of expectations and trust that you will get the guidance you need.

- ✦ If at any time you don't feel safe or decide you want to stop the reading, put your cards down and say *'The reading is finished.'* Clear yourself and your space and deck. Remember that you're in control and you get to decide who to connect with, how the reading goes and when it ends.

- ✦ If anything comes through that you are struggling to navigate on your own or you just want to talk about, call a friend or a professional medium who can help support you.

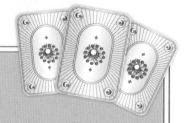

Pull a card!

Ask these questions:

✦ How could mediumship readings help and support me at this time?

✦ Is there anything I need to be aware of before I attempt mediumship readings?

✦ How can I best protect and prepare myself for this work?

Follow this process for a simple mediumship reading:

✦ Clear and prepare your space and energy.

✦ Set an intention that everything that comes through is in alignment with your best and highest good.

✦ Affirm you will be safe and protected in this space.

✦ Light a candle and invite in who you would like to speak with. You can do this simply by saying: '[Name], *thank you for coming through for me today and passing on any messages you have for me.'*

✦ Shuffle the cards while you ask them what message they have for you.

✦ Pull as many cards as you feel drawn to; sometimes one is all you need!

- ✦ Read the cards, journal, ask extra questions and do whatever else you need to do.
- ✦ Thank whoever it was you invited in.
- ✦ Clear yourself and the space and put your deck away.

CHANNELLING

Working with oracle cards can be a powerful gateway for activating your channelling abilities. There are many different types of channelling, from trance channelling, which occurs when the channel (the person doing the channelling) goes into a deep hypnotic trance and almost appears to become the deity, spirit or energy they are channelling, to simply channelling a short message or part of a message from your higher self or inner knowing. You've probably channelled already, since so much of what is received during readings is channelled information.

Channelling is sometimes misunderstood, but you don't have to give over your body or mind to channel. In fact, you can channel from a very conscious and aware state in which you have 100 per cent control at all times over what comes through and how you pass it on.

Some oracle decks lend themselves to channelling very well. The *Angels Among Us* and *Goddesses Among Us* decks or any other decks that feature angels, deities, gods, goddesses, ascended masters or other spiritual beings are great for this work. The cards can become a kind of anchor or doorway into connecting with the consciousness of that being.

Other types of oracle cards that depict an energy or object, for example a crystal, flower or landscape, can also be used. Instead of channelling a being you can channel the energy of what the card represents. If there's a place on the card you could channel the ancestors or spirits of that place, and you can channel by using symbols or images such as gateways or portals for higher beings to move through. For example, the image of a white feather can help you to channel angelic beings and a cross could help you to channel the saints.

Keep in mind that not everything and everyone needs or even wants to be channelled, and you may find you are only able to form a deep connection with certain deities or energies. Here are some things to think about before channelling:

✦ Do you already have a relationship with a particular being or energy? It will be much easier to channel if you have a good, strong relationship with them.

✦ Do you have complete faith and trust in this energy to bring you messages of only love, support and guidance?

✦ What are your intentions for channelling?

✦ Remember that no matter how good you get at channelling there are still things that can get lost in translation.

✦ Sometimes you might fall into the trap of thinking that because it's channelled it must be absolute truth, but even channelled messages can be personal for you or a small group of people and may not resonate with everyone.

✦ When channelling, only take what resonates with you and leave the rest.

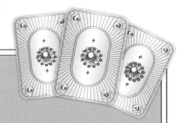

Pull a card!

Ask these questions:

✦ How could channelling support me on my spiritual path?

✦ How can I prepare myself for channelling?

✦ Who or what would be best for me to try channelling?

Channelling takes practice, so try working with this beginner's process at least a couple of times a week to help you develop this skill.

✦ Prepare your space and your own energy for a reading.

✦ Relax: you may like to take some extra time here to meditate and quiet your mind.

✦ Choose a card that depicts the energy you want to channel. When you're starting out, choose a card upright from the deck that depicts a deity, guide or energy you feel comfortable with and trust to guide you safely.

✦ Ask yourself what this being or energy would want you to know right now. Record in your journal as if the being or energy is speaking to you; for example, 'I want you to know that . . .' rather than 'This being wants me to know that . . .'

- ✦ Let your pen flow. Try to clear your mind, release any thoughts of how strange this is and just go with it. Record whatever weird and wonderful things come through even if they don't seem to make sense in the moment.

- ✦ When you're done go back over your notes. If it's your first time channelling you may find that not all of it makes sense. Look for the messages that feel important and really speak to you.

- ✦ As you get more confident in channelling you'll find the messages come through more clearly and you begin to intuit which messages are coming from your own monkey mind and which ones are really channelled.

Channelling through writing, or automatic writing as it's often called, is just one way of channelling. You can also channel through your voice. Try the same process as above but voice record yourself speaking instead of writing. You can do this with your eyes open looking at the card to help you or close your eyes and let yourself go into a more meditative state as you speak.

Remember that you always have the power to stop channelling at any time if you don't feel comfortable. All you have to do is open your eyes, close your mouth or put your pen down. Shake it off and do something else for a while.

READING FOR OTHERS

It can be a beautiful and rewarding experience to read for others. Most people start off reading for friends and family who are open and have some level of interest in spirituality, which is a good place to start as friends and family are usually very supportive. To do a reading for someone else:

✦ Set up your space. If you're at a friend's house or even a coffee shop this could be as simple as bringing out your reading cloth or just visualising the space around you being clear and protected.

✦ Prepare your energy: take time to clear, ground and protect yourself. If you don't have a lot of time you can just take a few deep breaths and visualise yourself in a column of light.

✦ Invite your guides in to support you. This can be a quick *'Thank you, guides, for being with me as I do this reading for* [person's name].' You can do this out loud or in your head.

✦ Set an intention that everything that comes through the reading is in alignment with the best and highest good of the person you are reading for.

✦ Ask the querent (the person you're reading for) for their question. If they give you a muddy question, lots of information or quite a few questions take a moment to talk with them about what it is they really want to know, then formulate a clear and empowering question for them.

+ Shuffle the deck and pick cards in the same way you would if you were reading for yourself. Some readers like to let the querent shuffle and pick the cards, while others don't let anyone else touch their cards. Do whatever feels right for you.

+ Lay down the cards and begin telling the querent about the messages you are seeing in the reading. As you go through the cards ask the querent if what you are saying resonates, because there's nothing worse than doing a whole reading only to have them say at the end that nothing made sense. Ask questions as you go along, and if you are off track you can reground and recentre and try again.

+ Always try to be empowering and supportive in your readings for others. Remind them that they have the power!

+ At the end of the reading ask the querent if they have any feedback on the reading.

+ Thank the querent and your guides.

+ After a reading always clear yourself and your space and cards.

PLEASE NOTE THIS IMPORTANT INFORMATION ABOUT READING FOR OTHER PEOPLE:

+ Always make sure you have willing participants.

+ *Never* read for someone, tune in to their energy or pass on any psychic or intuitive information without their permission.

+ Don't read for sceptics unless you really like a challenge!

+ Always focus on wishing the best for your querent.

Pull a card!

Ask these questions:

+ How could I serve and support others through oracle readings?
+ How can I best prepare myself and my energy for reading for other people?
+ What do I need to remember when reading for other people?

Reading cards for others is a big responsibility, and it's important you feel absolutely ready when you start reading professionally.

BEFORE YOU HANG UP YOUR ORACLE-CARD READING SHINGLE, CONSIDER THE FOLLOWING:

+ Are you able to hold space for people who may be going through trauma, grief and difficult things in their lives?
+ Can you put your own beliefs, politics and opinions aside when reading for someone who doesn't share the same views as you?
+ Can you be non-judgemental no matter what questions the querent brings to the table?
+ What your intention is for becoming a professional reader.

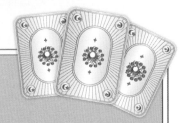

Pull a card!

Ask these questions:

✦ What do I need to know about reading cards professionally for others?

✦ What do I need to work on in order to read professionally?

✦ How could I serve and support others and myself by reading oracle cards professionally?

✦ How can I prepare myself for reading professionally?

There is no university degree in oracle-card reading, which means anyone with a deck can charge for readings. This is wonderful for those who are ready but not so great if you throw yourself in too soon.

To prepare for reading professionally do 100 readings in exchange for feedback. Yes: that means reading for 100 different people, most of whom ideally will not be known to you. As you go through this process a few things will happen:

✦ You'll get a lot of practice and get much better at reading for others – and yourself!

✦ The feedback you get will help you know what to work on.

✦ You'll begin to understand more about working with your own energy.

✦ You'll realise pretty quickly whether this is something you really want to do. If you burn out after 20 readings and decide you only want to read for friends and family or even just yourself from now on, great: do that! If you are super lit up, getting great feedback and don't want to stop once you hit 100 then start charging for your services, and good luck on the journey!

One hundred readings may feel like a lot, but this is your apprenticeship, your initiation into the role of an oracle. See it as a sacred process and a chance to really hone your skills and prepare you for the job. Try not to see this as giving away 100 readings and instead see it as an energy exchange: you're swapping your time and energy for feedback and on-the-job training.

> **Personal note:** when I started out reading for others I did 100 readings before I charged a cent. Doing this helped me to become a better reader, get paid clients, move into running New Age Hipster full time and quit my day job. Those 100 readings created a solid foundation that led me to being here today writing this book. There are no shortcuts on the magical path. If you really want to read for others and do this as your job then practise, practise, practise!

THE REAL ORACLE MAGIC

As you've discovered along this journey, oracle cards are an incredible tool that can help you to receive divine guidance and tune in to your inner knowing. If you don't do anything with that guidance your oracle practice will remain nothing more than just a bit of fun and a warm fuzzy feeling for the 2 minutes it takes to pull a card and consider its meaning.

If you're reading this book and you've come this far or you flicked ahead to this chapter, it's likely you don't want your oracle deck to be just a pretty object that sits on a shelf or maybe gets used on the odd full moon or when you have a big problem and need some divine intervention. You're here for the real deal, the real oracle magic.

The real magic of reading oracle cards happens when you listen to the guidance you get, do the inner work, show up and take action in your life. It is so easy not to do this. It's so easy to pull your cards, nod your head or roll your eyes at the messages and then carry on as you were. It can take a little extra from you to really start listening and paying attention, to bring the guidance with you through your day and start living a more conscious life. However, when you do *everything* can change.

You can be the most deeply intuitive and psychically connected person in the world and still not be able to do anything with your guidance or use it to create a positive impact in your life, or you can be someone who is just starting to get those intuitive hits but are already using them to create incredible change in your life and the lives of others.

IF YOU NEED A LITTLE HELP TO KICK-START YOUR REAL ORACLE MAGIC JOURNEY CONSIDER THE FOLLOWING:

✦ Start a daily spiritual practice, which can be like a mirror to your life. When you show up for your spiritual practice you'll find you also start showing up in so many other ways. Remember that this practice can be as short as 1 minute, but you must at least try to do it every day. If you miss a day then no worries, start again tomorrow, but there is immense power in showing up even for a few minutes.

✦ When you pull a card that suggests a change needs to be made, get clear on what that change is. Pull another card if you need to for clarity then make a plan to make that change.

✦ If you don't know how to start, pull a card and ask 'What is my next step?' When you get the answer and it feels right, take it. Take that next step, no matter how small, and see where it leads you. You don't have to change your whole life in a day; one small step each day will get you there.

✦ Don't be hard on yourself. If you ignore your guidance for six months before taking that first step, it's okay. You just had to get to the right place to be able to start. Self-love is so important on this journey.

✦ Ask your guides to help you!

✦ Focus on one small piece of guidance at a time. Pull one card at the start of the week then actively focus on that guidance as you go about your week. When you feel you're ready to move on, ask for the next piece of guidance.

- ✦ Get support: connect with a friend and do this work together. Find a Facebook group such as the Spiritual Journey Pitstop, ask for advice and support when you need it or work with a healer, reader or coach. You don't have to do this work alone.
- ✦ Love yourself through it all. No matter what happens, remember you are an incredible being of light and you are doing so well on this journey. If you weren't you wouldn't be reading this right now.

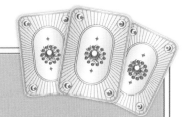

Pull a card!

Ask these questions:

- ✦ How can I trust and follow my guidance?
- ✦ What do I need to do to create lasting change in my life?
- ✦ What's my next step?
- ✦ How can I show up and make it happen?

NOTES

NOTES

ORACLE-CARD
READING
SPREADS

While a one-card reading is sometimes enough to shed a little light on a situation or offer general guidance and support when no specific question is asked, sometimes you really need to look at a situation in depth. Working with spreads can help you see things from a bigger and more-detailed perspective.

The spreads included in this chapter can be used with any oracle deck, and with tarot decks as well. In fact, any tarot spread you come across can always be used with your oracle cards.

Spreads usually have a specific theme, numbered positions and a question or prompt for each card. To work with a spread, simply prepare yourself for a reading, set your intentions and then shuffle the cards, placing each card face down in each of the positions of the spread.

When you're just starting out it can be helpful to turn one card over at a time so you're not overwhelmed by all the cards and their messages. As you gain confidence you may choose to turn all of the cards over at once for a quick overview before going back and reading each one individually. Once you've seen each card, take a look at how the cards work together: do you see any common themes coming up? For example, do you see both prosperity and abundance, or love and friendship? Do you see similar symbols or colours on the cards? Look for any similarities, common themes or messages that appear.

DOUBLING DOWN

If you feel as though you need extra guidance and support, pull two or even three cards for each position in a spread.

COMBINING DECKS

Try using two or more decks in a spread. Shuffle and lay the cards out with your first deck as you usually would, then take a second deck and repeat the process, laying the cards out above the first spread so you have two cards for each spread position. If you also read the tarot you can combine tarot and oracle decks as well as oracle and oracle decks.

CLARIFYING CARDS

If there's anything in your reading you don't understand you can always pull a clarifier card, which is an extra card or two you pull for more clarification. For example, if you don't feel like you understand the message in position two even after you've read all the other cards around it, you can shuffle your deck again and ask for more clarification. Pull a second or third card if needed to get more insight.

TROUBLESHOOTING

Here are a few things you can do if your spread still isn't making any sense:

✦ Go back to the questions from earlier on in the book. What's the first thing that pops into your head when you see this card? How does this card make you feel? Which elements of the card grab your attention? Go back to your decoding practice (see Chapter 3), noticing the colours, shapes, keywords, symbols and so on, and look for the hidden clues and meaning.

✦ Change the prompts: how you interpret the prompt in each spread position will be subjective and the language used may not quite work for you, your question or your deck. If you're confused about how the card answers the question in the spread, instead of trying to force it to fit take the card out of the spread and consider what it's trying to tell you on its own. If you need to, rewrite the prompt a little to make it fit for your overall question and the deck you are using.

✦ Journal: record anything and everything that comes up when looking at the card, even if it begins with how you feel frustrated that you don't know what it's trying to say. Sometimes this process can unlock and unblock you and help you to be open to receiving the answers.

✦ Let go of expectations: sometimes you'll get incredible card readings that feel like divine epiphanies, while at other times the process will feel more practical than magical. Trust that you'll get what you need however it comes through.

✦ Take a break: leave your cards out but do something else for a while. When you come back to the cards later you may be able to see something you didn't see before.

✦ Try again: if you really aren't getting it, not even a little bit, put your cards back in the deck, shuffle and draw again. Try to only do this if you really have to and never do it more than once in a reading. If you pull a second set of cards and it's still not making sense it's time to take a break and maybe revisit the earlier sections of this book.

CLARITY AND GUIDANCE SPREADS

BASIC THREE-CARD SPREAD

This three-card spread gives a simple overview of where you've been, where you are and where you're going. You can also look at this spread as what's behind you – what to leave in or learn from the past – what's currently on your mind or heart and what's in front of you. Remember that the future hasn't been written. This spread will give you some idea of where you may end up if you keep going on this path, but you can always change the outcome!

THE CARDS IN THIS SPREAD REPRESENT:

✦ **Card 1:** the past.

✦ **Card 2:** the present.

✦ **Card 3:** the potential future.

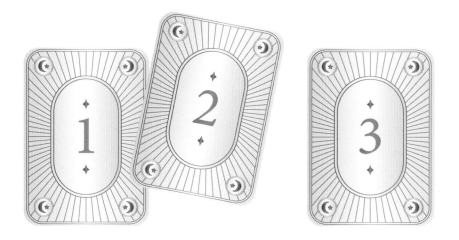

THREE-CARD ENERGY SPREAD

THE CARDS IN THIS SPREAD REPRESENT:

✦ **Card 1:** the current energy or situation.

✦ **Card 2:** what's influencing or affecting you positively or negatively.

✦ **Card 3:** how to move through it.

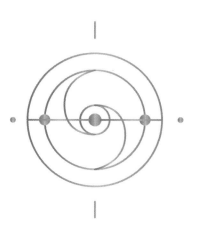

ADVICE, ACTION AND POTENTIAL OUTCOME SPREAD

THE CARDS IN THIS SPREAD REPRESENT:

✦ **Card 1:** the current energy or situation.

✦ **Card 2:** influences, blocks or challenges.

✦ **Card 3:** advice.

✦ **Card 4:** action.

✦ **Card 5:** the potential outcome.

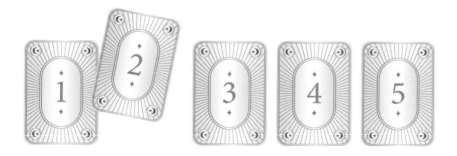

PERSONAL ENERGY CROSS SPREAD

Based on the first part of the traditional Celtic cross, this spread focuses on the energy within and around you. You can see this spread as a kind of full energy check-in to help you see what's going on in all directions.

THE CARDS IN THIS SPREAD REPRESENT:

✦ **Card 1:** the current energy or situation.

✦ **Card 2:** what's affecting you most right now.

✦ **Card 3:** what's below you, or what your subconscious is trying to tell you or what you're not aware of.

✦ **Card 4:** what's behind you, or lessons from the past and what to let go of.

✦ **Card 5:** what's above you, or new ideas and energy coming in. You could also read this as a general message from your guides.

✦ **Card 6:** what's right in front of you, or what you need to see or what you're not seeing.

✦ **Card 7:** what's further ahead, or the mostly likely outcome if you keep going in this direction.

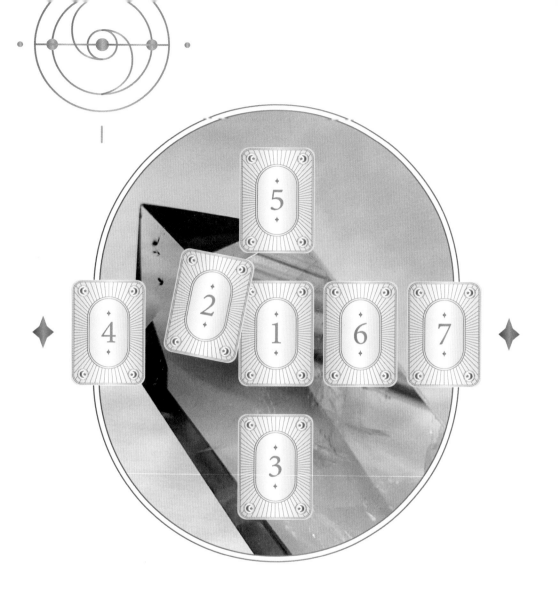

MAKING A DECISION SPREAD

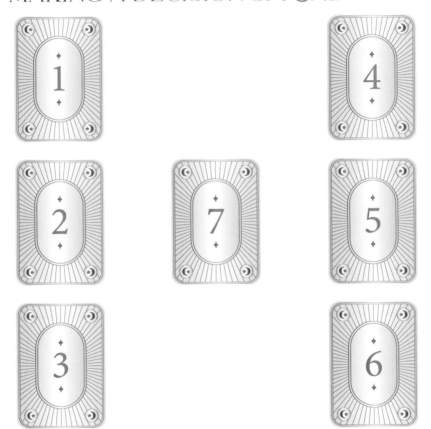

THE CARDS IN THIS SPREAD REPRESENT:

✦ **Card 1:** how option one could be good for you.

✦ **Card 2:** what challenges option one could bring.

✦ **Card 3:** what else you need to know about this option.

✦ **Card 4:** how option two could be good for you.

✦ **Card 5:** what challenges option two could bring.

✦ **Card 6:** what else you need to know about this option.

✦ **Card 7:** what you most need to know about this decision.

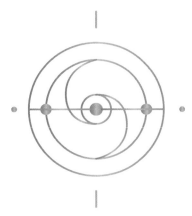

ASTROLOGICAL
SPREADS

NEW MOON MAGIC SPREAD

A new moon phase is a powerful time for manifestation, fresh beginnings and creativity. Try working with this spread before you do any new-moon magic or manifestation rituals. This spread works best from the point of a new moon and the proceeding three days.

THE CARDS IN THIS SPREAD REPRESENT:

+ **Card 1:** how to ground your magic.
+ **Card 2:** what to clear to make way for the new.
+ **Card 3:** how to connect with your power at this new moon.
+ **Card 4:** magic to make.
+ **Card 5:** how to surrender and trust.

WAXING MOON MAGIC SPREAD

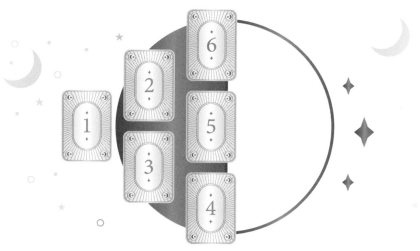

A waxing moon, when a new moon begins to grow and expand towards fullness, is a time to focus on your growth and expansion. You can do this spread at any point during a new and full moon.

THE CARDS IN THIS SPREAD REPRESENT:

✦ **Card 1:** what is stagnant and not moving forward.

✦ **Card 2:** what is blocking you.

✦ **Card 3:** how to get things moving again.

✦ **Card 4:** what needs to grow in your life.

✦ **Card 5:** how you can expand your own radiance.

✦ **Card 6:** how to continue to manifest your dreams.

FULL MOON MAGIC SPREAD

A full moon is a time of great spiritual and intuitive power, a time to give thanks, release, let go and power up your spiritual connection and psychic abilities. This spread works best from the fullest point of the moon to the proceeding three days.

THE CARDS IN THIS SPREAD REPRESENT:

+ **Card 1:** where you're at this full moon.
+ **Card 2:** what needs to be seen and known tonight.
+ **Card 3:** what needs to be released.
+ **Card 4:** what to call in and activate.
+ **Card 5:** intentions to be set.
+ **Card 6:** magic to be made.

WANING MOON MAGIC SPREAD

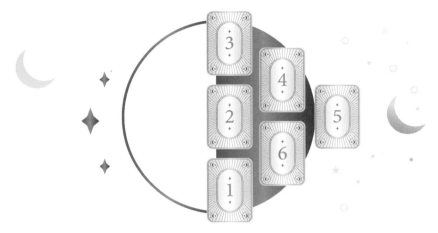

After a full phase the moon begins to wane, meaning it appears as if it's decreasing in size on its way towards becoming new again. This is a good time to continue to release and let go of what is no longer or never was working for you. You can work with this spread any time between a full and new moon.

THE CARDS IN THIS SPREAD REPRESENT:

✦ **Card 1:** what is no longer or never was working for you.

✦ **Card 2:** how to release it and let it go.

✦ **Card 3:** habits that aren't helping.

✦ **Card 4:** how to release those habits and let them go.

✦ **Card 5:** old stories and beliefs that aren't supporting you.

✦ **Card 6:** how to release those beliefs and let them go.

DARK MOON MAGIC SPREAD

A dark moon occurs just before a new moon in the space between the ending of a full moon and the beginning of a new moon. It's a powerful time for shadow work, to go deep into the subconscious and seek hidden wisdom.

THE CARDS IN THIS SPREAD REPRESENT:

+ **Card 1:** a message from your subconscious.
+ **Card 2:** what lessons are integrating.
+ **Card 3:** how to find peace in the darkness.
+ **Card 4:** what the dark moon is incubating.
+ **Card 5:** your guide through the dark moon.

MERCURY RETROGRADE SPREAD

Mercury goes retrograde around three or four times a year for about three weeks each time. As Mercury is the planet of communication, when it's in retrograde it can be useful to focus on clear communication and double-check everything before you hit send. But, mostly, this is a powerful time to pause, reflect and slow down, which is a wonderful gift a Mercury retrograde can offer us.

THE CARDS IN THIS SPREAD REPRESENT:

✦ **Card 1:** the energy you bring to this Mercury retrograde.

✦ **Card 2:** how the Mercury retrograde will potentially affect you.

✦ **Card 3:** inner work that needs doing.

✦ **Card 4:** how to rest and slow down.

✦ **Card 5:** what to re-evaluate.

✦ **Card 6:** what to rethink.

✦ **Card 7:** how to navigate through this time with ease and grace.

LOVE AND RELATIONSHIP SPREADS

KARMIC RELATIONSHIP SPREAD

Karmic relationships can be deeply intense and often come into your life to help you on your spiritual journey, to remember who you are and get you on your highest path.

THE CARDS IN THIS SPREAD REPRESENT:

✦ **Card 1:** why you are drawn to this particular person.

✦ **Card 2:** past-life influences.

✦ **Card 3:** lessons the person can teach you in this lifetime.

✦ **Card 4:** lessons you are here to teach the person.

✦ **Card 5:** how to grow and evolve together or apart.

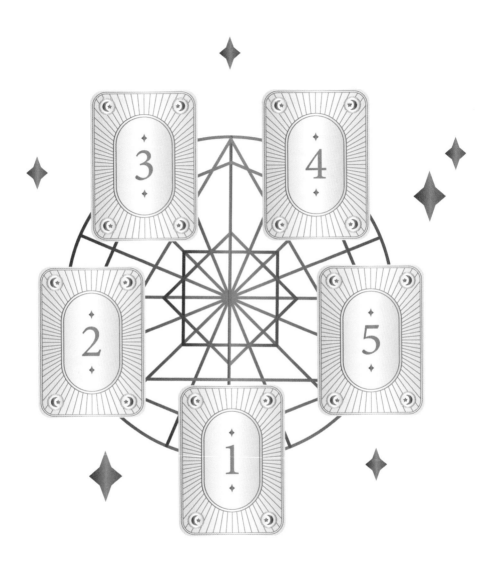

SOUL FAMILY SPREAD

Your soul family contains the people who feel like home or anyone you've had a strong bond with in this lifetime. You may have known people in your soul family in a past life or you could originate from the same soul group.

THE CARDS IN THIS SPREAD REPRESENT:

✦ **Card 1:** how to attract and call in your soul family.

✦ **Card 2:** how to recognise your soul family.

✦ **Card 3:** how to make yourself recognisable to your soul family.

✦ **Card 4:** how to love and support your soul family in this lifetime.

✦ **Card 5:** how your soul family will love and support you.

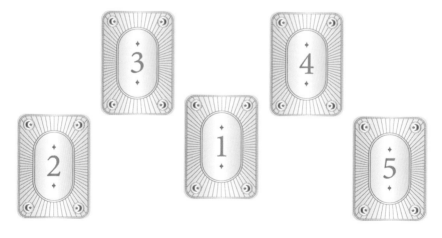

GREAT RELATIONSHIPS SPREAD

This spread can be used for all types of relationships: romantic ones, friendships or with family or even acquaintances and work colleagues.

THE CARDS IN THIS SPREAD REPRESENT:

✦ **Card 1:** what's working well in your relationship.

✦ **Card 2:** what's not working.

✦ **Card 3:** what you want.

✦ **Card 4:** what the other person wants.

✦ **Card 5:** an action to take to make things better.

BEST FRIENDS FOREVER SPREAD

THE CARDS IN THIS SPREAD REPRESENT:

✦ **Card 1:** what you bring to the friendship.

✦ **Card 2:** what your friend brings.

✦ **Card 3:** issues or concerns.

✦ **Card 4:** how to navigate through those issues.

✦ **Card 5:** how to honour and nurture the friendship.

✦ **Card 6:** how to stay friends forever.

DEALING WITH DIFFICULT PEOPLE SPREAD

THE CARDS IN THIS SPREAD REPRESENT:

✦ **Card 1:** why this difficult person has come into your life.

✦ **Card 2:** why you find this person so difficult.

✦ **Card 3:** what you can learn from this person or this situation.

✦ **Card 4:** how to protect your energy and set boundaries.

✦ **Card 5:** how you can bring love and compassion to this situation.

MOVING ON SPREAD

You can use this spread when you want to move on from a break-up, a friendship that has run its course or at any time you are moving on from something that is no longer working in your life.

THE CARDS IN THIS SPREAD REPRESENT:

✦ **Card 1:** what wasn't working.

✦ **Card 2:** lessons you've learned.

✦ **Card 3:** blessings to keep hold of.

✦ **Card 4:** how to return to yourself.

✦ **Card 5:** how to love yourself.

✦ **Card 6:** how to let others support you.

✦ **Card 7:** new adventures to go on.

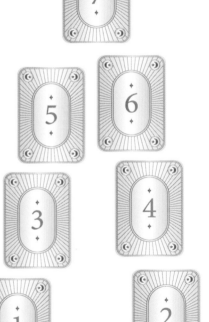

SPIRITUAL
DEVELOPMENT
SPREADS

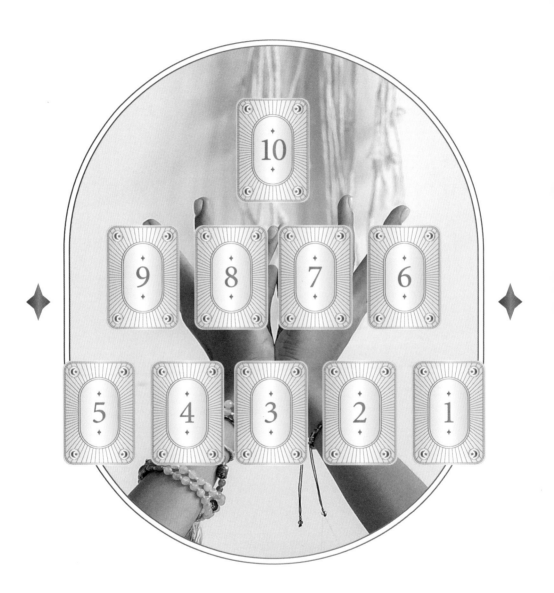

ORACLE CARD COMPANION

SPIRITUAL DEVELOPMENT SPREAD

THE CARDS IN THIS SPREAD REPRESENT:

✦ **Card 1:** an energy check-in.

✦ **Card 2:** what needs clearing.

✦ **Card 3:** how grounding will support you.

✦ **Card 4:** energy leaks.

✦ **Card 5:** your spiritual guide.

✦ **Card 6:** how you receive guidance.

✦ **Card 7:** how to develop your intuition or inner knowing.

✦ **Card 8:** how to develop your connection to source or divine guidance.

✦ **Card 9:** what to practise and work on.

✦ **Card 10:** a message from your guides.

PSYCHIC SUPERPOWER SPREAD

THE CARDS IN THIS SPREAD REPRESENT:

✦ **Card 1:** your psychic superpower.

✦ **Card 2:** how to clear psychic blocks.

✦ **Card 3:** how to activate your psychic ability.

✦ **Card 4:** how to use this power for good.

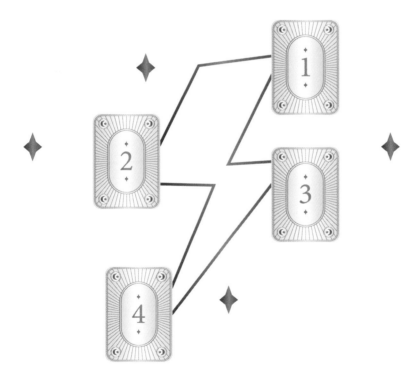

SPIRIT GUIDES SPREAD

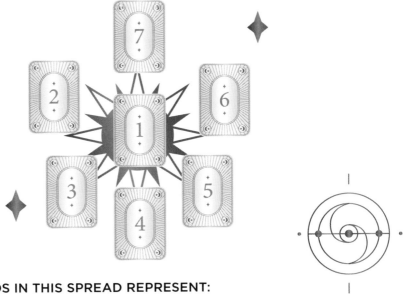

THE CARDS IN THIS SPREAD REPRESENT:

✦ **Card 1:** who your spirit guide is.

✦ **Card 2:** what they are here to help you with.

✦ **Card 3:** what they are here to teach you.

✦ **Card 4:** how you can hear them more clearly.

✦ **Card 5:** how you can develop a deeper connection with them.

✦ **Card 6:** anything else you need to know about your guide.

✦ **Card 7:** a message your guide has for you right now.

CONNECTING WITH YOUR ANCESTORS SPREAD

THE CARDS IN THIS SPREAD REPRESENT:

✦ **Card 1:** wisdom from the ancestors of earth.

✦ **Card 2:** wisdom from your ancestors by blood.

✦ **Card 3:** how to honour your ancestors at the altar.

✦ **Card 4:** how to honour your ancestors through action.

✦ **Card 5:** what to heal for your ancestors.

✦ **Card 6:** wisdom from your ancestors of spirit.

✦ **Card 7:** wisdom from your star ancestors.

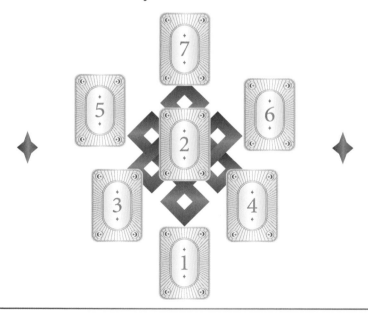

ANGELIC REALM COMMUNICATION SPREAD

This is a great spread to use with any angel-themed oracle cards.

THE CARDS IN THIS SPREAD REPRESENT:

✦ **Card 1:** a message from your guardian angel.

✦ **Card 2:** how to hear and see your angels.

✦ **Card 3:** how to communicate with your angels.

✦ **Card 4:** how to trust and surrender to the higher plan.

✦ **Card 5:** how to trust and surrender to higher love.

✦ **Card 6:** how to receive angelic help, support and comfort.

✦ **Card 7:** how to activate angelic frequencies and spread your wings.

DREAM INTERPRETATION SPREAD

THE CARDS IN THIS SPREAD REPRESENT:

✦ **Card 1:** why this dream came to you.

✦ **Card 2:** who or what sent this dream.

✦ **Card 3:** what your subconscious is trying to tell you.

✦ **Card 4:** what this dream was trying to communicate to you.

✦ **Card 5:** what to do with this dream and its message.

✦ **Card 6:** what you can learn from this dream.

✦ **Card 7:** how to bring this understanding into your waking life.

JOURNEY TO ENLIGHTENMENT SPREAD

THE CARDS IN THIS SPREAD REPRESENT:

✦ **Card 1:** how far along the path you already are.

✦ **Card 2:** what you've learned so far.

✦ **Card 3:** where you're struggling with the enlightenment journey.

✦ **Card 4:** what distracts you on the journey.

✦ **Card 5:** how you hold yourself back.

✦ **Card 6:** who or what can help you on the journey.

✦ **Card 7:** the next steps to take to move forward on this journey.

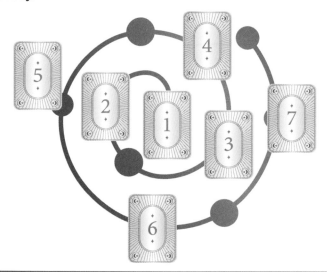

WITCH SPREAD

THE CARDS IN THIS SPREAD REPRESENT:

✦ **Card 1, earth:** how to take right action in the world.

✦ **Card 2, spirit:** a message from spirit.

✦ **Card 3, fire:** heart-led passions to pursue.

✦ **Card 4, air:** ideas and thoughts to pay attention to.

✦ **Card 5, water:** what your emotions are telling you.

LIGHTWORKER SPREAD

THE CARDS IN THIS SPREAD REPRESENT:

✦ **Card 1:** why you incarnated at this time.

✦ **Card 2:** how to activate the light within.

✦ **Card 3:** your personal lightworker mission.

✦ **Card 4:** how to achieve this mission and step up on the ascension ladder.

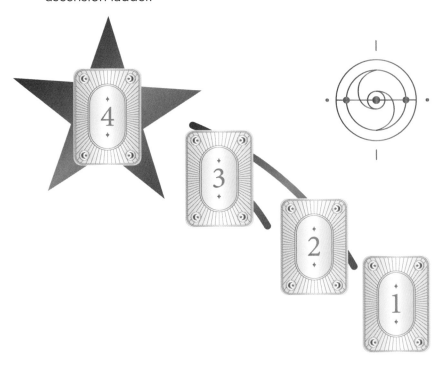

STAR SEED SPREAD

THE CARDS IN THIS SPREAD REPRESENT:

✦ **Card 1:** a clue to your star seed origins.

✦ **Card 2:** your galactic mission.

✦ **Card 3:** how to thrive on earth.

✦ **Card 4:** how to seed the light.

SPIRITUAL SEEKER SPREAD

THE CARDS IN THIS SPREAD REPRESENT:

✦ **Card 1:** what you are seeking.

✦ **Card 2:** what has already been found.

✦ **Card 3:** what to leave behind.

✦ **Card 4:** where to look next.

✦ **Card 5:** where and how the answers can be found.

SPIRITUAL
HEALING
SPREADS

GENERAL SPIRITUAL HEALING SPREAD

THE CARDS IN THIS SPREAD REPRESENT:

✦ **Card 1:** what needs healing.

✦ **Card 2:** the cause or root of this suffering or situation.

✦ **Card 3:** how this is affecting you and your life.

✦ **Card 4:** where to find healing and support.

✦ **Card 5:** how to allow and receive healing.

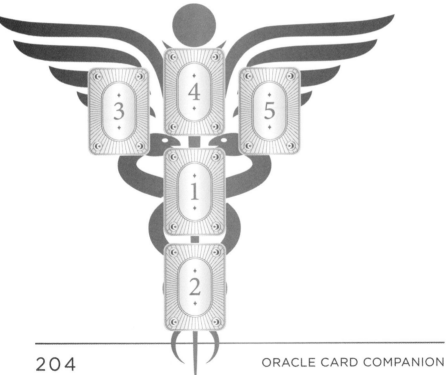

COMFORT AND SUPPORT SPREAD

THE CARDS IN THIS SPREAD REPRESENT:

✦ **Card 1:** what grounds you.

✦ **Card 2:** support from your guides.

✦ **Card 3:** support from the gods.

✦ **Card 4:** support from the goddesses.

✦ **Card 5:** support from your higher self.

✦ **Card 6:** how to honour where you're at.

✦ **Card 7:** action to take to help you through.

✦ **Card 8:** how to give yourself continued self-care.

CHAKRA SPREAD

THE CARDS IN THIS SPREAD REPRESENT:

✦ **Card 1, earth star chakra:** how to connect more deeply with the earth.

✦ **Card 2, root chakra:** how to ground into the truth of who you really are.

✦ **Card 3, sacral chakra:** how to create the life of your dreams.

✦ **Card 4, solar plexus chakra:** how to stand in your power.

✦ **Card 5, heart chakra:** how to love and be loved.

✦ **Card 6, throat chakra:** how to express your truth clearly and lovingly.

✦ **Card 7, third eye chakra:** how to see more clearly.

✦ **Card 8, crown chakra:** how to receive divine guidance.

✦ **Card 9, causal chakra:** how to brighten your halo.

✦ **Card 10, soul star chakra:** messages from your higher self.

✦ **Card 11, stellar gateway:** messages of the highest wisdom from source.

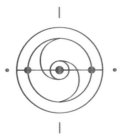

PAST-LIFE SPREAD

THE CARDS IN THIS SPREAD REPRESENT:

+ **Card 1:** who you were.
+ **Card 2:** why you chose to incarnate in that place and time.
+ **Card 3:** the main theme or lesson of your relationships.
+ **Card 4:** the main theme or lesson of your work.
+ **Card 5:** your greatest challenges.
+ **Card 6:** your greatest victories.
+ **Card 7:** how you died.
+ **Card 8:** karma you carried with you from that life into this one.
+ **Card 9:** the main lessons of that life.
+ **Card 10:** how this knowledge can help you in your current life.

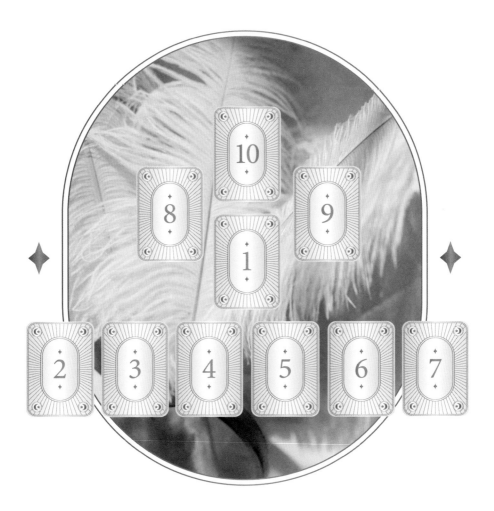

PURPOSE
AND WORK
SPREADS

LIFE-PURPOSE SPREAD

THE CARDS IN THIS SPREAD REPRESENT:

✦ **Cards 1, 2 and 3, your current purpose:** your purpose for today, this week and in the immediate future. These are short-term goals to help you fulfil your purpose right now.

✦ **Cards 4, 5 and 6, the purpose you are working towards over the next six months to a year:** think of these cards as your longer-term goals.

✦ **Cards 7, 8 and 9, your higher purpose or life purpose:** these are your goals for this lifetime.

CURRENT CAREER GUIDANCE SPREAD

THE CARDS IN THIS SPREAD REPRESENT:

✦ **Card 1:** your current work situation.

✦ **Card 2:** how this work is serving you.

✦ **Card 3:** how you are serving and supporting others through this work.

✦ **Card 4:** how to become more successful in this work.

✦ **Card 5:** new opportunities to be open to.

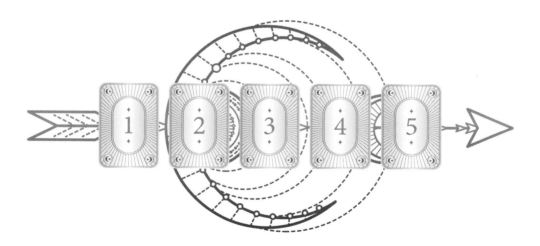

CAREER PLANNING SPREAD

THE CARDS IN THIS SPREAD REPRESENT:

✦ **Card 1:** your talents and abilities.

✦ **Card 2:** how you can help the world through your work.

✦ **Card 3:** work that could light you up.

✦ **Card 4:** career advice.

✦ **Card 5:** the first step to take.

✦ **Card 6:** longer-term goals.

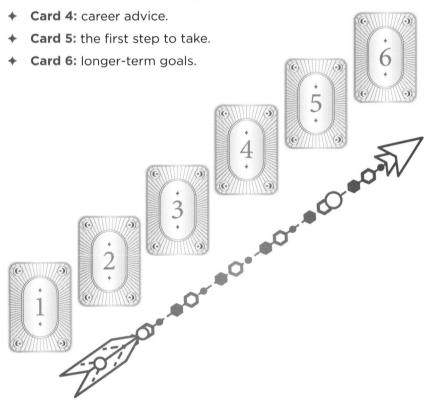

BIG DREAM SPREAD

If you like you can choose card 1 upright from the deck to symbolise your big dream if you already know what it is.

THE CARDS IN THE SPREAD REPRESENT:

✦ **Card 1:** your big dream.

✦ **Card 2:** a message from your guides about this big dream.

✦ **Card 3:** what's stopping you from living this dream.

✦ **Card 4:** how to align your energy to the frequency of your big dream.

✦ **Card 5:** how to attract opportunities that could bring your big dream closer.

✦ **Card 6:** how to meet the universe halfway.

✦ **Card 7:** a small step to take to get closer to your big dream.

✦ **Card 8:** a big leap to take to make it happen.

MONEY AND MANIFESTATION SPREADS

LAW OF ATTRACTION SPREAD

THE CARDS IN THIS SPREAD REPRESENT:

✦ **Card 1:** what you're attracting.

✦ **Card 2:** how you're attracting this.

✦ **Card 3:** what you want to be attracting.

✦ **Card 4:** what is blocking you from attracting this.

✦ **Card 5:** how to release these blocks.

✦ **Card 6:** how to attract what you want.

✦ **Card 7:** how to receive what you want.

CONSCIOUS MANIFESTING SPREAD

Do this spread before any manifestation rituals to make sure you're focused on calling in what you really want.

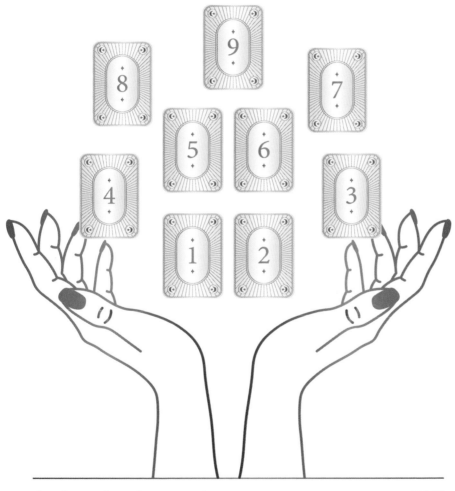

THE CARDS IN THIS SPREAD REPRESENT:

✦ **Card 1:** what your ego wants.

✦ **Card 2:** what your soul wants.

✦ **Card 3:** how manifesting this will change your life.

✦ **Card 4:** blocks that may prevent you from manifesting this.

✦ **Card 5:** how to release these blocks.

✦ **Card 6:** how to ask for what you want.

✦ **Card 7:** how to take action.

✦ **Card 8:** how to receive.

✦ **Card 9:** how to trust and surrender.

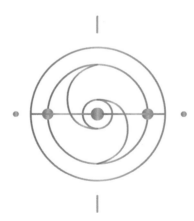

PROSPERITY CONSCIOUSNESS SPREAD

THE CARDS IN THIS SPREAD REPRESENT:

✦ **Card 1:** riches you already have.

✦ **Card 2:** how to bring in more wealth.

✦ **Card 3:** how to share the wealth.

✦ **Card 4:** how to feel rich here and now.

✦ **Card 5:** how to spend wisely.

MANIFESTING MONEY SPREAD

THE CARDS IN THIS SPREAD REPRESENT:

✦ **Card 1:** your current money situation.

✦ **Card 2:** your current money mindset.

✦ **Card 3:** beliefs and old stories that keep you limited.

✦ **Card 4:** spending habits that keep you limited.

✦ **Card 5:** new beliefs to cultivate.

✦ **Card 6:** how to be open to receiving.

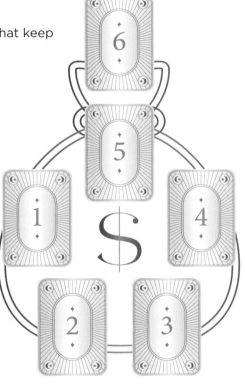

PERSONAL DEVELOPMENT SPREADS

SELF-LOVE SPREAD

THE CARDS IN THIS SPREAD REPRESENT:

✦ **Card 1:** why you're wonderful.

✦ **Card 2:** why people love you.

✦ **Card 3:** why your guides and ancestors love you.

✦ **Card 4:** how to see yourself through the eyes of those who love you.

✦ **Card 5:** one step to take on the journey towards more self-love.

✦ **Card 6:** a self-love practice.

✦ **Card 7:** how to keep on loving you.

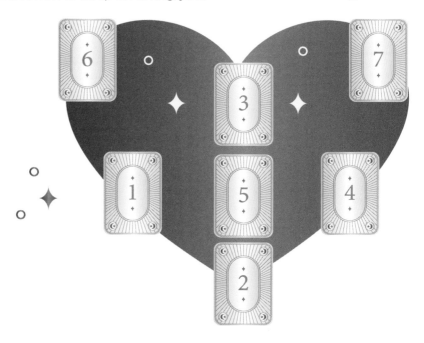

SELF-CARE SPREAD

THE CARDS IN THIS SPREAD REPRESENT:

✦ **Card 1:** where you are right now on your self-care journey.

✦ **Card 2:** why you need to cultivate self-care.

✦ **Card 3:** what blocks you from caring for yourself.

✦ **Card 4:** how to bust through this block.

✦ **Card 5:** old beliefs you have around self-care.

✦ **Card 6:** how to release these blocks.

✦ **Card 7:** what to stop doing to cultivate self-care.

✦ **Card 8:** what to start doing to cultivate self-care.

✦ **Card 9:** how to have more compassion for yourself.

✦ **Card 10:** how to honour the self-care journey of others.

✦ **Card 11:** a message from your self-care angel.

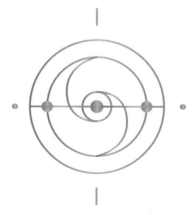

ORACLE CARD COMPANION

SHADOW WORK SPREAD

For more detail about shadow work, see Chapter 4.

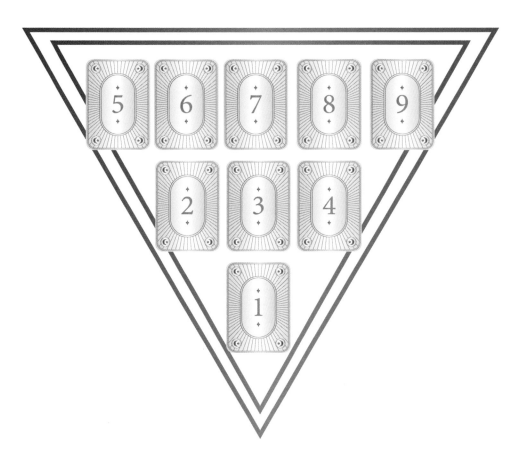

THE CARDS IN THIS SPREAD REPRESENT:

✦ **Card 1:** your current relationship with your shadow.

✦ **Card 2:** how to show yourself love while you work with your shadow.

✦ **Card 3:** where you may be projecting your own stuff onto others.

✦ **Card 4:** positive traits that are hidden and need to be remembered.

✦ **Card 5:** negative traits to work on.

✦ **Card 6:** what you need to take responsibility for.

✦ **Card 7:** how you may be self-sabotaging yourself.

✦ **Card 8:** what you need to acknowledge, accept and/or change about yourself.

✦ **Card 9:** how your shadow self can help you to live your best life.

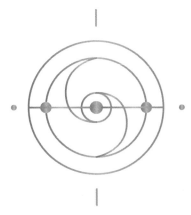

GRATITUDE SPREAD

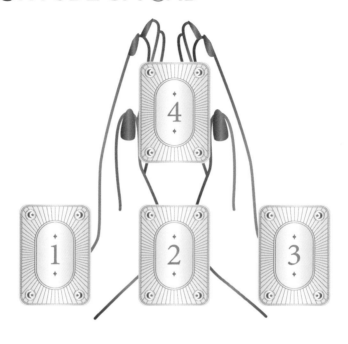

THE CARDS IN THIS SPREAD REPRESENT:

✦ **Card 1:** how and where to find gratitude.

✦ **Card 2:** what to celebrate.

✦ **Card 3:** how to honour yourself.

✦ **Card 4:** how to love your life.

WELL-BEING SPREAD

THE CARDS IN THIS SPREAD REPRESENT:

✦ **1:** who and what can support you.

✦ **2:** where to get support.

✦ **3:** why it's important to focus on your well-being.

✦ **4:** how to improve your well-being.

CREATIVITY SPREAD

THE CARDS IN THIS SPREAD REPRESENT:

✦ **Card 1:** what needs to be expressed and created.

✦ **Card 2:** creative blocks.

✦ **Card 3:** how to break through the creative blocks.

✦ **Card 4:** how to express the truth of who you are.

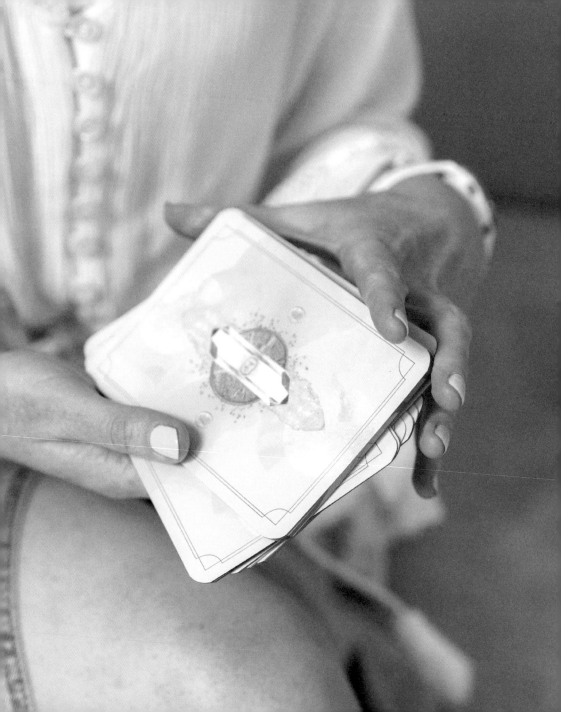

NOTES

FORTY DAYS
TO BECOMING
AN ORACLE

The 40-day journey described in this chapter is an accelerated pathway to becoming a more intuitive, confident and connected oracle-card reader. Ideally you will take this journey in 40 consecutive days, as a consistent practice really is the best way to see and experience results. If you do skip a day or if life happens then no problem: just pick up where you left off. Consider the following:

✦ Remember that this is your journey and these prompts are just suggestions.

✦ Listen to your intuition and make the prompts work for you.

✦ If you don't have time for the prompt, shorten it or do a quick one-card reading on that day instead.

✦ Trust yourself and your journey, and always feel free to go where you're guided.

▶ **Day 1.** Set an intention for what you want to gain from this 40-day practice then pick a card upright from your deck that symbolises this. Leave it out somewhere you will see it for the rest of the day or take a photo and make it your screen saver for the next 40 days.

▶ **Day 2.** Create a sacred space or altar in which to do your readings. See Chapter 1 for ideas on how to do this.

▶ **Day 3.** Work with the interview with your deck spread in Chapter 1 and get to know your deck.

Day 4. Read the information in Chapter 1 on who and what you are connecting with in a reading and figure out who or what that is. Invite this energy in and do a simple one-card reading for yourself.

Day 5. Practise clearing your energy (see Chapter 1 for more information). Once your energy is clear, do a one-card reading for yourself and record the process.

Day 6. Practise clearing and protecting your energy (see Chapter 1 for further information). Once you are clear and protected, do a one-card reading for yourself. Journal on the process and on your reading.

Day 7. Practise clearing, protecting and grounding your energy (see Chapter 1 for further information). Once you're clear, protected and grounded, do a simple three-card reading for yourself (see Chapter 5). Journal on the process and write about your reading.

Day 8. Prepare your energy for a reading, then try out different styles of shuffling to find out which one works best for you. Do a one-card reading for yourself with each shuffling style. Journal on each reading and the shuffling style used.

Day 9. Take some time to consider how you will formulate the questions for your readings. See Chapter 2 for some ideas on how to ask empowering questions. Prepare your energy for a reading, ask a clear empowered question and do either a one- or three-card reading.

Day 10. Answer the questions in Chapter 3 and begin to think about which of the clairs may be strongest for you. Take some notes and journal on your findings.

Day 11. Read Chapter 5 about working with spreads. Prepare your energy for a reading, then work with any of the personal development spreads in that chapter. Journal on your reading.

Day 12. Prepare your energy for a reading, ask a question then pull a card. Take some time to decode the card you pulled using the tips in Chapter 3.

Day 13. Do something today to practise developing your clairvoyance (see Chapter 3).

Day 14. Prepare your energy for a reading, then work with a spiritual development spread (see Chapter 5). Journal on your reading.

Day 15. Explore the pathworking exercise by taking a journey into your favourite card (see Chapter 3 for further information).

Day 16. Prepare your energy for a reading. Work with an astrology spread (see Chapter 5) that matches the moon phase you are in. Journal on your reading.

Day 17. Practise developing your clairaudience (see Chapter 3).

Day 18. Prepare your energy for a reading. Choose any spread from Chapter 5 and work with other spiritual tools such as crystals, oils and herbs to enhance your card-reading practice. Journal on your reading.

Day 19. Explore the pathworking exercise (see Chapter 3) by taking a journey into a card you don't feel a deep connection with.

Day 20. Prepare your energy and then work with a general spread (see Chapter 5) for guidance on whatever is most in your heart and mind right now. Journal on your reading.

Day 21. Practise developing your clairsentience (see Chapter 3).

Day 22. Work with the affirmation practice in Chapter 4 in the 'Manifestation' section. Say this affirmation every day for at least 11 days.

Day 23. Try out some energy healing with your oracle cards. Choose any energy-clearing practice from Chapter 1. Journal on your process and the results.

Day 24. Practise developing your claircognisance (see Chapter 3).

Day 25. Prepare your energy for a reading. Do a three-card reading for yourself using an empowering question and a connection with your clairs. Journal on your reading and on which of the clairs you feel is strongest for you.

Day 26. Chose a simple magic practice from the 'Magical workings' section in Chapter 4 and try it out.

Day 27. Prepare your energy for a reading. Work with any of the spiritual healing spreads in Chapter 5. Journal on your reading.

Day 28. Start exploring shadow work (see Chapter 4 for further information). Explore the prompts with your cards and in your journal.

Day 29. Call on a passed-over loved one and invite them to give you a message through the cards (see Chapter 4 for more information on oracle mediumship).

Day 30. Do a quick one-card reading for yourself and then undertake a little self-reflection. Journal on these prompts:

✦ How is your oracle card–reading practice going?
✦ What's going well?
✦ Are you finding anything difficult or frustrating?
✦ Are you feeling more intuitive or connected?

Day 31. Sit down for a chat with your ego (see the section 'Your ego' in Chapter 4).

Day 32. Practise channelling some higher wisdom through the cards. See Chapter 4 for further information on how to open up and start channelling.

Day 33. Prepare your energy for a reading then work with a love and relationship spread (see Chapter 5). Journal on your reading.

Day 34. Meet with your fears over a mug of cocoa (see the section 'Fear' in Chapter 4).

Day 35. Refer to the information on reading for others in Chapter 4 then try reading for a friend, family member or pet. If you have no willing subjects then do a reading for yourself. Journal on the results of reading for others or your own reading.

Day 36. Work with a manifestation practice from Chapter 4 and make something wonderful happen!

Day 37. Prepare your energy for a reading. Work with an astrology spread that matches the moon phase you are in (see Chapter 5) and journal on your reading.

Day 38. Prepare your energy for a reading. Work with a money and manifestation spread (see Chapter 5) and journal on your reading.

Day 39. Prepare your energy for a reading. Choose any spread from Chapter 5, using at least two cards per position with the same deck or two cards from different decks in each position. Journal on your reading.

Day 40. Celebrate yourself! Do something to honour yourself for how far you've come on your journey: post on social media with the hashtag #oraclecardcompanion, tell a friend or give yourself a gold star, or why not purchase a new oracle deck to celebrate? Prepare yourself for a reading and ask, 'Where to next on my oracle card–reading adventure?' Journal on your reading and how you feel at the end of these 40 days.

NOTES

NOTES

ABOUT THE AUTHOR

Victoria 'Vix' Maxwell is the creator of New Age Hipster, a spiritual home for good witches, lightworkers, star seeds and spiritual seekers. A priestess for the present time, modern mystic and spiritual teacher in Converse sneakers, she supports her worldwide community with reconnecting to their own light, inner guidance and power through soul readings, courses, online spiritual development circles, kundalini yoga workshops, podcasts, blogs and social media channels.

Vix is the bestselling young adult fiction author of the *Santolsa Saga* series, the author of *Witch, Please: Empowerment and enlightenment for the modern mystic, Manifest Your Dreams* and *Angels Among Us* and *Goddesses Among Us.*

To find out more about Vix head to www.newagehipster.co or follow her on Instagram, Facebook or TikTok: @newagehipster333.

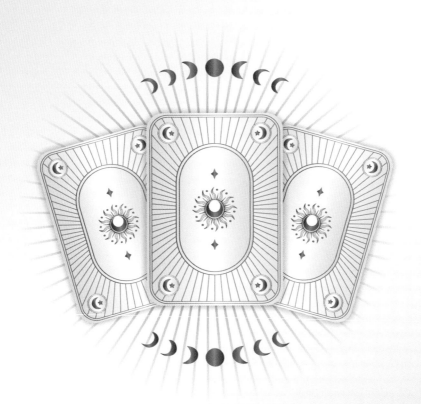

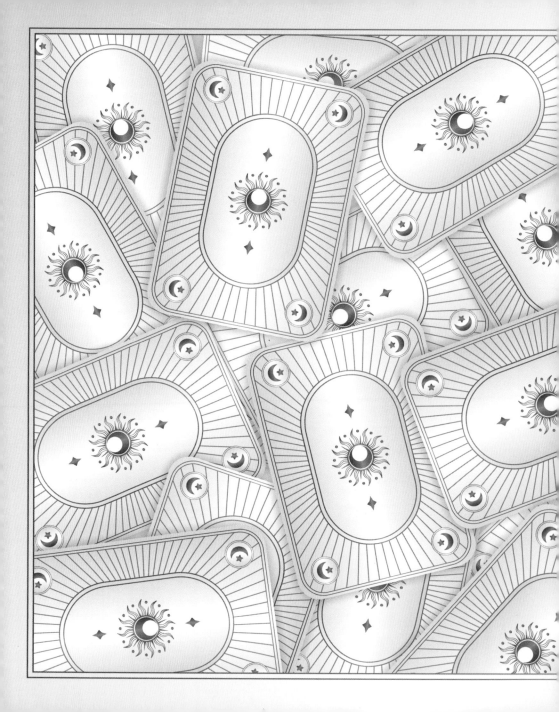